Urban Essentials 101

A Handbook for Understanding and Unleashing the Academic Potential in Urban Underperforming Schools

Julius R. Lockett

Bloomington, IN Milton Keynes, UK

authorHOUSE®

AuthorHouse™
1663 Liberty Drive, Suite 200
Bloomington, IN 47403
www.authorhouse.com
Phone: 1-800-839-8640

AuthorHouse™ UK Ltd.
500 Avebury Boulevard
Central Milton Keynes, MK9 2BE
www.authorhouse.co.uk
Phone: 08001974150

This book is a work of non-fiction. Unless otherwise noted, the author and the publisher make no explicit guarantees as to the accuracy of the information contained in this book and in some cases, names of people and places have been altered to protect their privacy.

First published by AuthorHouse 12/14/2006

ISBN: 978-1-4259-6061-2 (sc)

Library of Congress Control Number: 2006910264

Printed in the United States of America
Bloomington, Indiana

This book is printed on acid-free paper.

In honor of my father, Rev. Julius L. Lockett

...And he shall be like a tree planted by the rivers of
water, that bringeth forth his fruit in his season; his leaf also shall
not wither; and whatsoever he doeth shall prosper... (Psalms:1)

<u>Table of Contents</u>

Introduction

On January 8, 2002, Public Law 107-110, popularly known as "No Child Left Behind" (NCLB), was enacted by the Congress of the United States. The law, which was publicized by President Bush as a means of closing the achievement gap between underperforming urban poor minorities and whites, was ushered in with great optimism and fanfare. My initial reaction, however, was mixed. On one hand, I wanted desperately to share the enthusiasm and optimism. To think that after nearly one hundred and fifty years of efforts to improve the quality of education among urban youth, there was a possibility that there could finally be an effective solution to this languishing academic dilemma certainly energized me. On the other hand, my level of pessimism and cynicism was also ignited. I recognized from history and personal experience that past legislative and judicial acts had done very little in the way of improving the academic plight of urban minority groups, and, quite frankly, I harbored a theory that explained the lack of progress. Needless to say, I was rather perplexed. Should I be hopeful about this new legislation, or should I follow my normal course of suspicion, doubt, tacit approval, and reluctant acceptance? Realizing that I was far from being influential enough to alter the course of the debate, I concluded that President Bush, who advertised himself as a "born-again Christian" and a "compassionate conservative," deserved a chance. So I embraced the effort. But now, after more than four years of hopeful expectation and marginal returns, I have reached a very different conclusion.

Although NCLB was developed with the best of intentions, I am sorry to report that it is just another pipe dream. It's no different than the countless other gallant but misdirected governmental efforts of the past that were purportedly "researched" and then summarily thrust upon desperately optimistic parents in poor communities throughout the country. These parents—who only sought a better life for their children and a way for them to break free from the long-standing American oppressors of poverty, discrimination, ignorance, and greed—deserved better. But why didn't they get better? Why so much failure? I believe that the answer can be found in antiquity.

In all probability, most people are not as interested in history as I am. However, in order to better understand the failure and why I have taken a less-than-favorable position on NCLB, a brief historical chronology is in order.

The American public school movement has a rich socio-economic and multicultural heritage dating back to the early 1600s; however, the dominant influence on its structure and composition was largely shaped by the relationship between blacks and whites following the Civil War. After the freeing of slaves in 1865, the process of Reconstruction began. For the most part, Reconstruction, as far as northern politicians

1

were concerned, meant reestablishing a harmonious geopolitical relationship with the South. For southerners, it meant rebuilding their war-torn states. And at the same time, in spite of the glorious expectations of the Thirteenth, Fourteenth, and Fifteenth Amendments, it further meant getting back to the customary practice of oppression and discrimination. For the ex-slave, however, it didn't mean Reconstruction at all. For the newly freed blacks, it meant an attempted construction of a life for the first time in 246 years. And, even more menacing for blacks, it meant a forced association with their ex-masters who were now by law supposed to embrace them as fellow citizens. In a span of only of thirty-one years, because of a lack of compliance and the resulting intolerance and bigotry, the Supreme Court was obliged to address the subject in the Plessey vs. Ferguson decision.

In this 1896 case, the Supreme Court concluded that separate accommodations were legal. "Separate but equal," or Jim Crow, became the law of the land. As a result of this decision, our neighborhoods, churches, restaurants, restrooms, and, by default, schools were acutely affected. If implemented fairly, although it still would have been quite unusual, Jim Crow might have been feasible. However, as any astute eighth-grade social studies student could tell you, things were indeed separate, but they were conspicuously not equal.

Even though the court passed judgment and rendered its verdict of "separate but equal," state and local political officials guaranteed their white constituencies, and kept their promise, that the unbalanced system of favoritism would continue. Higher wages and the better jobs were typically given to the favored group. Restaurants and other businesses catered to the dominant faction and, in many cases, excluded minority groups altogether. So, naturally, public school systems were no exception. In some cases, the schools of the privileged groups were accommodated with public tax dollars by a margin as high as eight to one. As a result, Jim Crow was a great failure; however, it was not because it wasn't sufficient, but because it wasn't fair.

In the South and to a lesser degree in the North, segregation in public school accommodations was the norm. Most would say that this segregation caused blacks to receive inferior educations, but that's not exactly how I see it. A large number of blacks received what I would describe as a superior education. After all, this segregated arrangement was the same system that created and produced the most powerful group of black American leaders in history. Individuals such as George Washington Carver, Madame C.J. Walker, Langston Hughes, James Weldon Johnson, Thurgood Marshall, Rosa Parks, and Martin Luther King, Jr., were all products of the Jim Crow system. Nevertheless, to right this perceived injustice, the unanimous verdict by the Supreme Court in the 1954 case of *Brown v. Board of Education of Topeka, Kansas*, became the new substitute liberator.

The question before the Supreme Court was simple: Is segregated education detrimental to black students and thus unconstitutional? In light of the Fourteenth Amendment, which afforded all citizens equal protection under the law, and after the brilliant legal work of Thurgood Marshall, and the assumed poignancy of Dr. Kenneth Clark's doll study, Chief Justice Earl Warren and his colleagues were left with but one logical conclusion. Segregated schools were harmful, and, hence, unconstitutional. A year later, because most jurisdictions were not complying with the ruling, the courts held a second hearing where they ordered that the injustice be righted with "all deliberate speed." The *Brown* verdict overturned the fifty-eight-year-long reign of Jim Crow. Judicial verdicts, however, are given birth to with relative ease in the conceptual hallowed halls of justice, but on the concrete streets of reality, old customs and traditions die hard.

Both *Brown* decisions were met with serious resistance. In the South, the phrase "with all deliberate speed" was so bastardized that it eventually became synonymous with "never." This failure by southerners to comply with the court's decision eventually led to another well-meaning but failed effort: forced integration.

The most memorable and publicized case of forced integration took place in Little Rock, Arkansas, in 1957. The students, who became known as The Little Rock Nine, were forcibly integrated into Little Rock's Central High School amidst serious, even violent, protest. In this instance, then-governor Orval Faubus refused to comply with a federal court order that obligated him to admit nine black students to the all-white school. When Faubus refused to comply, President Dwight D. Eisenhower, using his executive powers, sent federal troops to enforce the order. These specific students went on to graduate, but in general, most southern schools remained segregated. This unrelenting breach of the law became a major catalyst for the civil rights movement of the sixties.

The civil rights movement was media-dominated primarily by Dr. Martin Luther King, Jr. One of the movement's high points occurred in 1963, when Dr. King and others marched to Washington, DC, to encourage the government to fulfill its promise of equality. Most leaders, however, believed that equality was to be achieved via integration. At the March on Washington, Dr. King spoke with luminous oration to a crowd estimated at more than 250,000 and imparted his illustrious dream for America.

The March and other non-violent protests led to the Civil Rights Act of 1964. Like the *Brown* decision of a decade earlier, this was another act of good intentions. The directive was designed to abolish racial discrimination in employment, public accommodations, and voter registration. With this act in place, after it was signed into law by President Lyndon B. Johnson, the black South believed itself to be moving in the direction of full liberation. However, in Atlanta, Georgia, one of the hotbeds of the movement and the city of my birth, desegregation was still virtually nonexistent.

In 1962, I entered Pryor Street Elementary School, an urban-poor, underperforming public school. In spite of all of the legislative language, judicial rhetoric, and executive orders, each and every face in the place—students, teachers and staff—was black. In Walter Leonard Parks Middle School and George Washington Carver Vocational High School, all the way to my graduation in 1975 (with the exception of a couple of teachers and one white boy who lasted about a week with his attempt to single-handedly desegregate Carver High), the schools remained segregated and continued to underperform.

One of my older brothers tried integration through busing. But that didn't last too long. Part of the well-documented problem with busing was that it was unfair and unjust. The common cliché was that the buses ran in only one direction, from our neighborhood to theirs. So in order to participate in integration, kids from our neighborhood had to be willing to go outside of the community in order to receive a "quality" education. After a very short stint, my brother and many others promptly learned that it was far safer to take their chances in our dangerous "hood" than in their "quality" environment and promptly transferred back to their neighborhood schools.

As an adult, I talked with my brother about his experience at the newly desegregated, white-dominated Central Junior High School of Atlanta. According to my brother, he was taunted, heckled, and threatened daily, and was even beaten up a few times by the older boys. He also believed that the teachers were racist. Although they didn't make racist comments directly to him, they appeared to furtively condone the behavior of the assaulting students.

Since it was assumed that busing would be the wave of the future for urban public schools, a course of well-documented white flight soon followed. This departure left behind huge gaps in funding for inner-city schools. Even the traditionally white schools that had been compulsorily desegregated were left in a position similar to that of their black counterparts. To remedy this problem, President Johnson, as part of his plan for a "Great Society," declared "War on Poverty." However, a lack of financial support brought on by the exorbitant cost of the Vietnam War lead to a serious under-funding of the program, and this became the new explanation for the failure of urban underperforming schools.

When we arrived in January 2002, the urban education issue was clearly unresolved. President Bush recognized it and made an effort to resolve the issue of underperformance with NCLB. Some might argue that NCLB was nothing more than a political maneuver, but I have found absolutely no reason to believe that the President was being anything less than honorable. I believe that President Bush recognized the value of an educated populace and set out to achieve it. I further believe that he was very clear about the needs of urban underperforming students. I also believe that the President and his brain-trust fully understood the goals, objectives, product design, and expectations for NCLB. But I also believe that, like his predecessor, Mr. Bush had no inkling about what it would take to create a viable system for urban underperforming schools. Therefore, by default, we got more of the same.

Although I have already stated that I believe NCLB to be just another pipe dream, a brief examination of its components should be undertaken.

Under NCLB, there are ten titles that are designed to bring about a change in public education as we know it. The ten-pronged strategy is listed below:

TITLE I—Improving the Academic Achievement of the Disadvantaged

TITLE II—Preparing, Training, and Recruiting High-Quality Teachers and Principals

TITLE III—Language Instruction for Limited English Proficient and Immigrant Students

TITLE IV—21st-Century Schools

TITLE V—Promoting Informed Parental Choice and Innovative Programs

TITLE VI—Flexibility and Accountability

TITLE VII—Indian, Native Hawaiian, and Alaska Native Education

TITLE VIII—Impact Aid Program

TITLE IX—General Provisions

TITLE X—Repeals, Redesignations, and Amendments to Other Statutes

The entire document is voluminous. (If you feel inclined to read through it, the government web address is www.ed.gov/legislation/ESEA02/)

As you can see by the titles, NCLB's focus is to correct a problem identified as prevalent among the urban poor and underperforming minority groups. Just as with the prior legislative interventions, I have a problem with this approach as well. The problem I have is twofold. First, as with all of the previous initiatives, there are no guarantees that it will yield results. And, even more pointedly, there are no consequences for the program's creators for its failure. If we take this approach, the legislators can continue to play the shell game with urban underperforming schools forever. Secondly, all of the corrective measures under NCLB are directed towards teachers, principals, students, and the schools themselves. This approach makes the assumption that they are the problem. It also creates a ripe environment for the traditional train and blame game: fashion the problem, create the programs, train the participants, and, without including the participants in the formative process or determining whether the strategies created were even right for their circumstance, blame them for the failure of the program.

Over the past ten years, I have participated in scores of academically-strategic training sessions and professional development workshops. Some of the workshops I genuinely thought were philosophically brilliant, but totally wrong for the urban underperforming environments where I worked. So, focusing heavily on professional development and strategically training teachers is shortsighted at best. Or it may be a tactic unto itself. The training may serve as a means for certain political and administrative officials to avoid stating the obvious—that they don't have an answer to the crisis. But whether it is shortsighted or deliberate, I will offer no further discussion of the NCLB legislation. I'm more interested in presenting my solution than highlighting their possible political *modus operandi*.

Relationships and Resources

I believe that success in urban, underperforming, public schools comes down to two over-arching principles or themes: ***Relationships and Resources.*** I further believe that we will not realize sustained positive growth in urban underperforming schools until the two are solidly established simultaneously. Then, and only then, will urban underperforming public schools rival high performers all over the country.

Currently in underperforming schools, the overwhelming majority of the focus is on the resource side of the model. We tend to think that money and/or using money to acquire books and materials, the latest pedagogical strategies, and certificated or "quality" teachers is the answer. We never stop to consider whether the materials and strategies are relevant for their intended audience or whether the teachers can forge real relationships with the students and the community. The reason that we never investigate this arena is simple. Most of the policy-makers come from environments where this relationship component is a natural part of the communal landscape. Consequently, they structure the politics of urban education around their experience and their frame of reference. This one-sided version of education leaves them practically blind to the fact that relationship formation precedes academic acquisition. This one-sided version of the predicament leads to flawed reasoning. It is this flawed reasoning that invariably leads to flawed policies and programs. And as a result of the flawed policies, we continue to get a cookie-cutter, one-size-fits-all program approach to education. The program inevitably focuses first and foremost on the best instructional practices that money can buy, to the detriment of the best relationships that people can build.

If we take a look at the majority of failing urban public schools and compare them to higher performers, some being separated by as few as five or ten miles in distance, it is easy to see that the high performers have both—relationships and resources—intact and working for them. Students who attend the high-performing schools generally have more stable family relationships and a more involved community. The parents are inclined, and better able, to financially support their schools, and they (the students and their parents) identify with and support their teachers on a multitude of levels—racially, socially, educationally, financially, and, in many cases, even religiously. Their relationships are unbroken, and that makes all the difference. The dissimilarity graphic below may help to explain the notion and impact of the differing relationships.

Teacher – Student Dissimilarity Graphic

Urban Underperforming Schools	High-Performing Schools
←————————————	————————————→
Resources but _no_ relationships	Resources _and_ relationships
Teacher-student _lack of_ familiarity	Teacher-student familiarity
Relationship deficient	Relationship rich
Arrogance (false self-image and esteem)	**Self-esteem**
Low buy-in, low standard performance	High buy-in, high performance

A   **M**   **Z**

Domain of the Urban Student   *Domain of the Average Teacher*

From the dissimilarity graphic, it is easy to see that urban underperforming students come from and tend to relate best with persons with experiences from environments A through M. On the other hand, the majority of teachers tend to come from and relate best with persons with experiences from environments M through Z. Because of this variance in experiences, a serious relationship disparity is often the result. This detail is neither presented as a mechanism for justifying behavior nor blaming a specific entity or group. This condition holds true for both urban and rural settings. It simply highlights the reality of the situation. When this variation occurs, the likelihood of high academic performance in any environment is extremely unlikely. In order to bridge this gap, there are only two viable alternatives: hire more teachers with A to M backgrounds and experiences or teach the existing teachers and staff to relate with students from A to Z.

History illustrates that, when it comes to the urban underperforming schools, we have tried a host of combinations and methods, but we have yet to try to forge a system based on Relationships and Resources. We've tried Jim Crow, or relationships without resources; we've tried busing, or resources in the midst of broken relationships. And in California, we have tried keeping the students in the underperforming community schools, importing teachers, and throwing enormous sums of money at them without cultural acquaintance or relationship-building. These efforts have all produced very little in the way of positive, measurable results. I think it's time for us to combine Relationships and Resources into one doctrine.

The relationship component deals with the normal interactions that naturally occur in a stable community. Normal relationships include the customary respect extended from a child to its parent, the routine and ordinary positive interactions between children, and the traditional courtesy normally extended to professionals—doctors, lawyers, teachers, and members of the clergy. Currently, many urban underperforming schools are suffering from a lack of common folkways, nonexistent or scattered ethical and moral traditions, a collision of cultural experiences, and poverty. These types of fractured environments create prime conditions for conflict, chaos, and strife. NCLB makes no provision for these relational-based entities. Sure, each and every school district's education code is required to have, and enforce, a discipline plan; however, referrals, suspensions, and expulsions are not the answer to a problem as complex as this. If we expect to see real, measurable improvement, we must rebuild, or in some cases construct for the first time, traditional social relationships in resource-rich environments throughout this country's urban public school system.

I don't know how to insure that available financial resources are allocated fairly. Perhaps the true work for legislators and justices is the guaranteeing of an equitable distribution of funding while the work of relationship-building is left to a different set of experts.

This book is about the development and implementation of a high-quality teacher-student relationship program in urban underperforming public schools. It is about hiring and preparing teachers to become expert urban underperforming school relationship builders. This text will identify and discuss five elements—***the student, the environment, discipline, instruction,*** and ***the teacher***—that are key to the understanding and building of solid relationships within urban public schools.

This book is written for teachers, school administrators, and government officials who would like to try a fresh yet time-honored approach to truly building a just and equitable system for all of America's youth. Further, it is written as a practical alternative to the status quo and as a catalyst for real change. This book is written for urban parents who have worked and waited too long and received too little in the way of positive results. Finally, this book is written for those students in urban underperforming schools who are being systematically impeded from a genuine opportunity to attain the necessary skills to achieve the elusive American dream.

The Student:

a) Who Are They (Portrait of a Student)
b) Sanity, Insanity, and Common Sense
c) Self Esteem vs. Arrogance
d) The YMCA Model (SMB)
e) The 3Ts

Julius R. Lockett

Who Are They? (Portrait of a Student)

Perhaps the most vital ingredient in the relationship-building process and, thus, the process of turning around underperforming schools, is knowledge of the student. As a teacher (and member of the school staff), you must know your students individually, collectively, socially, and academically. I know that this admonishment is issued as part of the general rhetoric in most teacher education programs, but in the case of urban underperformers, it must be taken much more seriously. This section will focus on providing a means for identifying and, more importantly, relating with urban underperforming students, both socially and academically.

On any given day, in varying degrees, there are usually three types of students in an urban, underperforming, public school classroom: **Long Shots, Straight Shots, and Sling Shots.** The division of students within these groups will more often than not determine the level, and relative ease, of information dissemination within the classroom environment.

More often than not, in each and every urban underperforming classroom throughout this country, there are students who are there, whether consciously or unconsciously, to disrupt and destroy the designed flow of the learning process. This group, to its detriment, consists of those students who have decided that the system, as established, is not working for them, and therefore they are not working for or with it. When students reach this point, they are mentally far removed from the level of receptiveness necessary to receive the full benefits of the educational process. It is because of this separation and distancing that I call this group the *long shots.* The second group is *straight shots.* They are the conformers. These students, regardless of the social and academic barriers erected, will wholeheartedly buy into the structure of the program and successfully navigate it, without objection and with few missteps. The final group I call the *sling shots.* The slings are the swing group. They are the students who will ultimately decide the direction of the class. They are the middle-of-the-road, "lukewarm" folk that can be persuaded to go either way. It should go without saying that it is the teacher's knowledge of, and ability to relate with, all three groups that is almost the exclusive determinant over the direction and course of the classroom. A graphic diagram illustrating this collective typology is displayed on the next page.

Student Typology

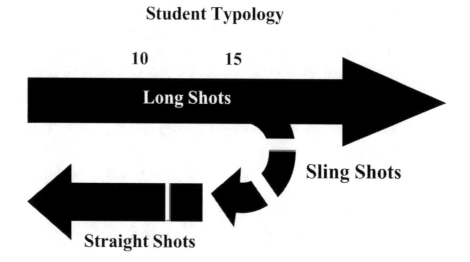

(The numbers above the diagram represent the ages of the students. The long shots are represented by the solid line beneath the numbers. The straight shots are represented by the bottom left-pointing arrow with the single break. The break represents the group of students that are transitioning from sling to straight or from straight to sling shot. The sling shots are represented by the curved arrow with multiple breaks. The multiple breaks represent the uncertain directional nature of this group.)

Genuine *long shots* are normally an extreme minority in a classroom, but in an urban underperforming school, they may be two or three times the norm. These students have spent, in some cases, as many as fifteen or sixteen years developing and perfecting their strategies of self-destruction, disruption, and undermining themselves and the instruction process. They are the wannabe gang-bangers, "plastic pimps," counterfeit rappers, and imitation lovers; they are the abnormal attention seekers, the frequently truant, and the serious classroom management problems. They are the students who act hardcore on the outside, yet are the most inwardly fragile of the three groups. They need to feel as though they are in control, yet don't have enough adult savvy to seek control in a constructive, acceptable fashion. Their aggressive, negative behavior is a defense mechanism, even though they display it as offense. Long shots are the guys and gals who are in your face, not because you have necessarily done anything out of the ordinary to provoke them, but because you haven't established yourself relationally as someone deserving of their respect.

Establishing yourself with the long shot is a very serious matter. I've been in workshops where teachers have been instructed to ignore the long shots and to not make a big deal about their behavior. That strategy is ridiculous because the long shots are usually testing the environment to see just how safe they are going to be in your domain. To convince them, you have to establish yourself as someone who can be trusted to look out for them in a moment of serious distress. In other words, they need to know if you are hard enough or skilled enough to protect them. If they conclude that you can't do the job, this group will take your class away from you and exploit it to protect themselves.

And they'll fight like hell to keep it. So if you are the classroom teacher, which in their eyes is synonymous with leader, and they sense fear or reluctance on your part when a situation arises, even with them, and you fail to rectify that situation, they will go for a power grab. For them, it's the same game that takes place on the streets among cliques, sects, and gangs every day.

When the power grab is complete, it's extremely difficult to recover. Long shots are fierce defenders of their perceived power. Once they are in charge, your lessons are doomed to failure, and the environment, in general, will be decimated by them. In the aftermath, they will publicly discuss with other students how they destroyed you and your efforts, which may lead to years of hell-raising, disruptions, and chaos in your classroom. I know this group intimately, because I was one of them.

Long shots usually, but not always, come from fractured homes. There can be one or both parents present, but in many cases they are either too busy to, don't know how to, or simply don't monitor, support, and promote mainstream values like traditional discipline and academic accomplishment. That is, the parents don't necessarily believe that education is vital, or they don't know how to instill the value of accomplishment through education. When this devaluation of traditional success occurs, the long shot usually replaces it with an abstract principle like personal respect, defined on their terms.

Respect is usually the measure of accomplishment for a long shot. Respect is the long shot's status, esteem, and protection. It serves the exact same purpose as self-esteem for high-performing students. But abstract principles such as respect, hate, and prejudice can become dangerous when long shots are left to determine their meaning. When a long shot defines a principle such as respect, he usually inserts a dose of delusion and paranoia, which distorts the essence. When this happens, it becomes the flash point of his existence and something to be defended wherever necessary, including your classroom. Some of the worst brawls I've ever witnessed arose from a presumed slight stemming from perceived disrespect. It is this fractured existence, coupled with the failure to attain traditional discipline and academic achievement, which often leads to the embracing of warped abstract principles in the life of a long shot. This distorted condition often makes fundamental matters like respecting the rights of others, working in cooperation with the establishment, and going to school on a regular basis a major challenge.

For instance, when I was navigating my way through the long-shot seas, I stayed in the ghetto with my mother during the week and in the suburbs with my dad on most weekends. I'm certain my mother thought good grades were important, because she would verbally say so. But for some reason, she was too busy to follow up on her statements. She never checked my homework or checked to see if I even had any. So it was easy for me to slide right into the comfort zone of a solid long shot. It started in elementary school, when I got out of control and didn't get checked at home for the behavior. Sure, the corporal punishment (1960s-style butt-whippings) tempered me some; but when that stopped, I was unleashed. I was suspended from school so much that my mother finally surrendered altogether. By the time I was in seventh grade, I was a major knucklehead and a devout truant. In my mind, school was distorted into something for squares and lames. Almost every day, instead of going to school, I would hang out with my friends at somebody's house, eating, drinking cheap wine, smoking pot, and having sex with girls who were gullible enough to participate. In my warped eyes, I was a player. Having fun and feeling protected by the crew, I was respected.

Like me, a lot of long shots come from the ghetto, and in the ghetto, idols are everything. The primary idols are athletes and entertainers, drug dealers, petty criminals like gamblers, burglars, thieves, and knockout artists (great fighters). The problem with having those guys as idols is that they usually didn't give a damn about school. They didn't care at all about which teachers had credentials, they didn't care about the latest instructional methods, and they certainly didn't place much emphasis on whether an individual is considered a highly qualified teacher (HQT) by incomprehensible, ambiguous NCLB standards. They focused on the relationships.

In my hood, there were teachers who were legendary. Mr. Banks, Mr. Fussell, and Mr. Neison (in elementary school), and Coach C.C. Jones, Coach Clarence Fisher, and Coach Erskine Bozeman (in high school) were such relationship builders that they became a part of the fabric of the community. They were so entrenched in the community that even today, more than thirty-five years later, when talking with someone from my old community, it's difficult to have a conversation without mentioning them. Those teachers had reputations for connecting and developing relationships with the students first, and then teaching them. Those guys were so well established in the community that you knew about them even before you started school. If the topic of "good" teachers ever came up, and sometimes it did, the older knuckleheads would tell you which teachers were HQT in their opinion. But being good, in their eyes (and I concur), had nothing to do with instructional methodology. It was all about the relationship, rapport, leadership, respect, and connection, and then instructional ability. (Attributes of effective teachers will be discussed later, in the section on the teacher.)

Connection and protection are everything to the disconnected long shot. And it's easy to see that this is true; just look at them. The long shots, even more than corporate executives, yearn to belong and feel a part of something. And they are just as easy to spot. They imitate what they value with even greater exaggeration than the genuine article. If a true long shot is going to sag, he's going to be the saggiest sagger in Sagville. If he is going to idolize a rap artist, he imitates the dress, walk, talk, dance, and the struggles. He'll rap with an audience or while walking alone; he'll even rap out loud in your classroom while you're trying to teach.

Why do the long shots imitate their idols? For the same reasons that business executives do: they hope to duplicate the success, and it doesn't matter whether the success is viewed as mainstream or questionable. From their perspective, what their idols have accomplished is far more real and attainable than chemistry and physics. They imitate for bravado, popularity, and as a compensation for their lack of intellectual competence. I call this intellectual compensation the smokescreen effect: act the fool, and nobody gets to challenge you on an academic level. It's all about connection and protection. However, regardless of the reason, just know that unless you control it, long shots are going to be in the classroom participating actively in a game that they are good at—creating chaos.

Although long shots are the ultimate groupies, they usually don't emulate individuals that they see as weak pencil-pushers. It's not the geek peddling some pie-in-the-sky college degree with whom they identify and align. It's the non-intimidated, back-in-your-face, vocal, and visible people that capture their attention. Please be clear! I'm not advocating violence. If a crime is committed and violence is needed, that's what the police are for. I'm advocating individuals who are not afraid to stand firm. I'm advocating leaders and campus legends. Yet even with that reality staring them right in the face, school administrators and officials continually spend their time recruiting people with whom *they* identify or relate instead of people who identify with the urban underperforming student. If you want to see an immediate change in failing public schools, recruit more former long shots as teachers. They are the people who have, against all odds, overcome the adversities and know how to successfully engage the long-shot system.

Please be mindful that I'm not saying we don't need teachers who are academically and instructionally prepared. I am most certainly of the belief that they must be. What I am saying is this: sometimes we miss the point, and we do things with good intentions that net poor results. A prime example of this was desegregation. The assumption was that black kids needed greater opportunities to excel, and that it could be accomplished by putting them in "better schools" with "better teachers." This was to be accomplished by busing them out of poor neighborhood schools. The end result was supposed to be better instruction, a better environment, higher self-esteem, and ultimately mass emergence from poverty via education. But what we really got was something totally different. The reason for this failure was simple: a misdiagnosis of the problem. And it was ethnocentricity and xenophobia that led our government down that wrong path. The real problem was the fact that schools were "separate but *not* equal." Students at white schools had it all. Teachers had a connection with their students, and they had the built-in protection that usually comes with homogeneity. They had relationships. And without going into the details, they also had the resources to implement their plan their way. Busing black students into white communities was merely a trade-off. The black students were given the resources, but the connection and the protection were severed. And that severing of the relationship explains a great deal about the low achievement of underperforming minority groups today. The students are not dumb! They have merely become fragmented or void of connection. This disconnection places them in a state where they imitate and attempt to connect with almost anything that is contrary to the establishment. It is the resurgence of the connection that will best eliminate the problem of the long shot.

Having said this, the ultimate question becomes how we can maximize the potential and minimize the negative effect of the long shot in the classroom, right now. I believe that there are a number of ways to achieve positive results and reduce or eliminate the long shot's effect. I'll briefly discuss two.

The first thing that could be done has already been mentioned. The most expedient way to nullify the long shot's effect and achieve a positive outcome would be for district administrators to put more former long shots in direct contact as teachers with the students. Even though I recognize this as the most expedient solution, I don't believe this approach will be implemented. The reason is this: most administrators were not long shots. As I stated earlier, most of the people in authority really prefer to select and hire individuals with whom they can identify and are similar to them. Once hired, these persons are elevated to positions of power, and they are reluctant, skeptical, or sometimes even afraid to deal with the ex-long shots themselves. So with this preference-based bias in effect for teacher recruitment, I think this first option is unlikely.

The second more viable option is teaching the current teacher and staff population how to relate with, manage, and counteract the long shots. The most logical candidate for providing this instruction is someone who is an ex-long shot. This person could be inserted into the staff development workshop schedule, preferably during the summer, in order for the new teachers to be prepared with a plan prior to being thrown into the lion's den. The summer is also a good time for implementation because a great deal of time will be needed in order to enlighten teachers and change their current thinking about the psychology of discipline. (This issue, and the problems surrounding it, will be discussed later in this chapter.) This process would take some time, but it could transform urban public schools forever.

Like the long shots, the **straight shots** are also small in number. I will not spend much time on the straight shots, and I hope that you won't either, because they don't need it. There are usually about as many straight shots as there are long shots in an average classroom. But in an underperforming school, the straights may constitute an even smaller group. In general, straight shots are the antithesis of the long shots. Unlike the long shots, however, the straights often come from homes where education is really appreciated, esteemed, and cherished. They come from homes where the parents oftentimes refuse to relinquish their offspring to the shallowness of "pop culture" and so-called psychology experts. Straights generally come from environments where substance takes priority over trend and flash, and even though many of them may live in poor or ghetto neighborhoods, they are usually non-participants in the ghetto life. In short, the straight shots come from homes where the walk and talk are scholastically synchronized. They are the students who are bound for college whether the teacher comes to work or not.

So what can teachers do to enhance the environment for the straight shots? They can do two things: minimize the long-shot effect and then simply get out of their way.

As much as you would like to show off the latest in-service and professional development strategies, restrain yourself when dealing with the straights. Give them help only when they ask for it. The second and most important thing that a teacher can do to assist the straight shots is to learn not to set them up. In other words, don't mount a target on them that the long shots can zero in on. The straights already know they are smart. But being labeled the smart guy in an urban underperforming school is like being set up like a neon sign on an isolated road. It is also too tempting for the long shots to resist taking potshots. The straight shots know it. So if you raise them up and the long shots start gunning for them, because they are smart, straights will figure out a way to divert the incoming fire, and this diversion could be detrimental to them and to you.

As a student and as an educator, I have often laughed when a teacher who has no skills for counteracting the long shot tries to turn to the straights for help. The teacher usually tries the old reverse psychology tactic. It's the one where an announcement is made with great pomp about how on-task a particular straight shot is. It's usually followed up with something like, "Why can't you be more like Richard or Sofia?" Immediately, the straights start to research their exit strategy because, over the years, they have made the connection between the superfluous adulation and the incoming fire from the long shots. Then they adjust accordingly. Ultimately, the whole plan backfires. The straight shot begins acting more like sling shots in order to take the pressure off, leaving the condition worse than before. So don't set up your straight shots.

The third and largest group of students to be found in any public school classroom is the **sling shot**. These are the middle-of-the-road folks. In many ways, they are the only accurately designated individuals in the classroom; they are true apprentices, students, or learners. The only question becomes, who will they learn from? Sling shots are the students who, for whatever reason, are undecided about which way to go. They are the ones who initially wait to see which direction the class is headed before pledging their allegiance. If the long shots prevail, the sling shots will ally with them, and that class will become pure, unadulterated hell for the teacher for the entire semester. If there's not a serious recovery, that class may potentially be ruined for the year and, in extreme cases, for the teacher's entire career because the word spreads. But if the teacher prevails, the slings will usually move in the direction of the straight shots. (Note that I didn't say that they will ally with straight shots, because that is very hard to do. The straights aren't vying for new members. They are usually very selective about the people allowed into their inner circle, and a lot of that has to do with their parents.) The obvious question becomes, how does one get the slings to align with the teacher? The answer ought to be just as obvious: control the long shots.

As I close this section, there are two points that I believe worth highlighting. In order to be an effective teacher, you must know your students, and once you know them, you must control the long shots. A second and loosely tied point is an admonishment directed to public school administrators. Actively recruit former long shots; they can work with all of the students. They are the only group of people out there who has legitimately traversed all three student types to some degree.

Sanity, Insanity, and Common Sense

Identifying the three types of students found in a public school classroom is merely the starting point on the way to knowing the students. At this point, we only know who they are. Now it's time to probe deeper.

In order to really find out where the students are behaviorally and psychologically, you must first make some sort of generalized assessment of them beyond long shot, straight shot, and sling shot. In order to do this, you must either know them experientially or spend some quality time getting to know them personally.

If you don't share a similar experience by assimilation (race, culture, socio-economics, or environmental similarities), it is imperative that you pursue a relation via acculturation or association. This is a huge task, and it is especially daunting when taking into consideration that most teachers don't live anywhere near the urban, poor, underperforming schools that they teach in, and, further, when you consider that most of them have no vested interest in the underperformer's success. But if there were a system that valued this association, the next thing that would need to be done is to expend some time and effort developing assessment tools for the task. These tools would assist in the evaluation of any information collected. You could create your own tools or you could use something that is already available. When I was in the classroom, I used a simple, informal rubric that I developed based on a characteristics continuum taken from a brilliant text that I read in the late 1980s entitled *Sanity, Insanity, and Common Sense: The Groundbreaking New Approach to Happines*s (Suarez, Mills, and

Stewart, 1987). Sometimes I collected data in a scientific manner, but mostly it was informal. After all, I wasn't accumulating this information as part of some esoteric exercise; the information was to be used immediately for relationship-building.

In *Sanity, Insanity, and Common Sense*, the authors lay out a continuum of what they call the "Characteristics of Conditioned and Unconditioned Frames of Reference." The continuum ranged from the highest to the lowest levels of consciousness. At the highest levels of consciousness, individuals are thought to be motivated by an unconditioned state of mind; while at the lowest levels, motives stemmed from a conditioned state. Atop the highest level of unconditioned characteristics were love and appreciation, and at the bottom, or lowest level of conditioned characteristics, were hate and prejudice (Suarez 119). Using these criteria, I came up with the following scale as a general means of evaluating my students. This scale is not to be thought of as an all-encompassing tool to be used for determining and explaining all of the complexities of human psychology. It is simply a generalized reference device that I use as a method of making common-sense assessments of the students in underperforming classrooms.

Student Typology by Characteristics

Love, Appreciation, Generosity,
Kindness, Gratitude, Compassion,
Patience, Understanding, Creativity,
Insight, Sense of Humor,
Satisfaction

Contentment, Security, Self-Esteem,
Cooperation, Flexibility,
Responsibility,
Motivation, Interest, Ability to
Concentrate, Productivity,
Achievement, Motivation,
Competition

Self-Image, Ego, Arrogance,
Seriousness, Commiseration,
Impatience, Frustration,
Boredom, Restlessness,
Dissatisfaction, Defensiveness,
Conflict,
Misunderstanding, Blame,
Judgment, Self-Righteousness,
Stress, Burnout, Anxiety,
Inefficiency, Emotional Instability,
Sadness, Anger, Hostility, Revenge,
Paranoia, Prejudice, Hate

Straight Shots Sling Shots Long Shots

Note that there is a spillover between groups, as no individual fits conveniently into rigid categories. For example, some sling shots will share traits with both long and straight shots at the same time.

Oftentimes, in order to get students to become more self-aware and to invite them to start thinking about their behavior and actions, I use this device as a class warm-up. When I introduce the graphic chart for the first time, I will generally take as much as an hour to explain it in detail. After the initial introduction, I try to use extracts from the model as often as possible as a daily warm-up. Without insulting their intelligence, a few days each week I will select diametrically opposing characteristics like paranoia and trust, blame and responsibility, or, one of my all-time favorites, boredom and creativity, and try to highlight them for the students by simply suggesting the possibility of there being a different way of thinking.

Using boredom, I explain how it is not an external but an internal force. So whenever students want to call a class boring, it is really a reflection of their lack of creativity. Think about it. All of the things you ever really got involved in required a certain level of interest, and it's the same way with class work. I think a huge problem in underperforming schools is that the administration puts too much pressure on teachers to be entertaining, and what they don't realize is that they are inadvertently making the students less creative.

I know someone is already thinking there is no time to implement something as detailed as this in a one-hour course and its follow-ups, while others are thinking I am wasting valuable instructional time on unrelated subject matter. My response to both of these concerns is this: if the classroom is in such turmoil during the instructional hour that you only get to really instruct about one-quarter of the time anyway, isn't the possibility of stabilizing the group worth this small investment? Also, when considering that all of the other so-called disciplinary measures and methods of the last twenty years have failed miserably, the time invested here is miniscule, and, thus, easily justified.

Self-Esteem vs. Arrogance

In every single urban underperforming school where I've worked, I have observed a common theme. Instead of teaching students to acquire real self-esteem, they have been pumping them full of conceit and haughtiness, which, left unchecked, leads to arrogance. I don't think it's a coincidence.

By the time the students have finished elementary and middle school, they're well on their way to becoming little egomaniacs. This naturally leads me to believe that instead of being rooted and grounded in true self-esteem, somewhere during that time period these students are being fed a constant diet of falsehoods about their self-importance, which leads to arrogance and narcissism. They are not being honored, admired, esteemed, or venerated because of their accomplishments; they are being rewarded for nothing, and in some cases for less than nothing. Take social promotion, for example. The districts that practice this travesty swear that they are making an effort to preserve the student's self-esteem; but in reality, this behavior only feeds the ego, which leads to arrogance. The students quickly learn that it doesn't matter what they do because they still get to move ahead. This move-on-no-matter-what mentality assists them in the idiotic notion that they're bulletproof. They quickly reason that there is no need to improve. There is no obvious incentive to do so or immediate penalty for failure. It's backwards thinking. Allow me to speak from experience. During my ninth-grade year, I went to school only when I felt the urge to make a cameo appearance, and as a result, I was retained one year. Boy! I felt terrible. I was so humiliated that I went to summer school, took four classes, got all A's, got in the game, skipped the eleventh grade, and graduated with my regular class. If I had been a victim of social promotion, I would never have known the authentic joy that comes from genuine accomplishment (self-esteem). The same thing goes for grade inflation. Students know when they've done nothing to pass a class. So when you pass them along, they don't see you as being cool; they see you as being easy, a weak trait in urban settings.

I also believe that much of the misguided affirmation is media-driven. One example that I frequently use to illustrate this point is the song, "The Greatest Love." For several years, that song was standard fare at primary and secondary graduation and awards ceremonies. The lyrics begin:

> "I believe the children are our future; teach them well, and let them lead the way. Show them all the beauty they possess inside; give them a sense of pride."

I have no real issues with that part of the song, although pride can be a two-edged sword. But where I do take serious issue is when the song instructs:

> "I decided long ago never to walk in anyone's shadow. If I fail, if I succeed, at least I did as I believed. And no matter what they take from me, they can't take away my dignity."

First, we should be encouraging students to walk in others' shadows; we call this shadow-tracking, mentoring. Also, a student's success should never be left solely to that person doing as he or she believes. And lastly, the song deliberately attempts to build up esteem without accomplishment, confusing esteem with arrogance. Sometimes it is necessary to put aside pride and dignity in order to see and hear the truth, accept it, and build anew. I think students all over California, and possibly throughout the country, have taken songs like these and made them their mantra. As a result, the norm for urban underperforming schools has become seriously dissipated and full of debauched, self-serving behavior. Why not? After all, we told them ourselves not to conform to our standards.

There is one other point I would like to make here. There is a current trend in my school district of blaming the teacher for the student's failure. I have actually heard administrators unequivocally state that if a student didn't reach competency in a subject, the teacher wasn't engaging enough and if several students failed a class, there was a problem with the teacher's methodology. In other words, they would rather point the finger at the teacher than challenge the student to strive for the excellence that leads to true self-esteem.

This practice of blaming the teacher is so widespread that even the students understand it. In a history class that I taught several years ago, a student challenged me on my interpretation of how the game of school is played. While I was teaching at ALBA, a zero tolerance school for the suspended and expelled, a newly-arrived student told me, in an exceedingly arrogant and haughty manner, that at his previous school he had been in an Honors History class and that I was requiring too much for my regular class. After assessing his skill level, I saw clearly that the honors designation was just another phony method of self-esteem building. At the end of my class, the student earned a "C." Prior to leaving ALBA, the student approached me wanting to revisit the issue of Honors History. In our conversation, he actually admitted that he thought the honors class he was taking at his old school was pretty weak too, and that he had tossed the title around because he had gotten a lot of mileage out of making his status known. In parting, he told me that he was proud to get the "C." He further said that he was now confident he could go back to his old school, put forth some real effort, and actually become an Honors History student. This student was well on his way to reaching genuine self-esteem.

We must rebuild our relationships with urban underperforming students on a foundation of honesty, humility, and submission to quality leadership. We must teach the students to be meek and not settle for academic mediocrity. The place to start is at the core of their being. We must go back and teach them what it means to be human.

The YMCA Model (SMB)

Before I tackle this section, I want to make it clear that I neither advocate nor endorse the teaching of a particular religion, or any form of religious proselytizing, in public schools. However, as a credentialed history teacher, I do think it is of historical and cultural significance for students to know about the various religions of the world. So when I present the YMCA model here, I am not presenting it as an endorsement of Christianity or any other faith or creed.

When making an effort to reintroduce students, or in some cases, introduce students for the first time, to themselves, I use the YMCA model—*spirit, mind, and body*. I chose it for two reasons. First, when I was a kid, my brothers took me to swim at the downtown YMCA in Atlanta. Being from the ghetto, I was so impressed with the facility that I tried to soak in every detail about the place. One of the things that stuck in my mind was the neon sign outside that consisted of a triangle with the words "Spirit, Mind, and Body" running along its axis. As a youngster, I pondered its meaning, but only in a fleeting manner. The second reason that I use the model is because as a young adult, I ended up working at that same YMCA as a lifeguard. At that point, I gave their philosophy considerably more thought. However, the thought that I gave it wasn't religious but humanist-based. I wanted to know if there actually were three components to humanity.

There was no debate about the mind and body, so I spent my time and effort exploring the spiritual issue. After examining the tenets of many of the major religions (Buddhism, Christianity, Deism, Hinduism, Islam, Judaism, Taoism, and even Zoroastrianism), I then turned to the philosophy of humanistic theorists like Sigmund Freud, Abraham Maslow, B.F. Skinner, and others. After this inquiry, I concluded that many of the philosophers also believed in a human composite that went far beyond the mind and body. Take Freud, for example. He is considered the father of psychology, yet was known to be a great reader of religious materials. He was also known to quote the Bible. Freud introduced the notion of the id, ego and super-ego, which were invisible or abstract forces of the mind. These forces are presumed to influence behavior. If Freud's theory is plausible, why couldn't there also be a totally separate and distinct abstract force which is designed to dramatically influence our character? After my exploration, I concluded that what we come to understand as spirit is perhaps that force.

I also concluded that the opposition to the notion of the spirit in this country is more of a constitutional issue than a scientific conflict. The vast majority of people use the abstract third part of the trio in discourse all the time. We simply settle for words like "conscience," "morality," "character," "principles," "ethics," and "scruples." But regardless of what we call it, the implication is the same. Spirit implies something beyond the common controls of the mind. Spirit, then, is just another name for our conscience, character, morality, or ethics; and from my observation, it's just not readily observable on a large scale in most of the underperforming students whom I've encountered.

Students in urban underperforming schools where I've worked seem to insist on functioning via the mind and body only. After thinking about it, I understood why. Simply put, they have no other frame of reference to call upon. As I watched the students, it was easy to see that they spent a great deal of their time contriving and forging ego-driven notions. The efforts often resulted in confrontations to justify their misplaced logic. And the confrontations often disproved their beliefs, sometimes with tragic results. But because there were no other forms of reasoning to call upon, they continued along the same cycle. In other words, their egos are writing checks that their bodies must try to cash, and oftentimes they can't cover the overdraft. These students clearly need to learn how to call on something other than their egotistical prejudices to resolve their issues. They need desperately to integrate their full human capacity. When full humanity is realized, they will be able to build more effective relationships with others. To accomplish this, whenever I taught urban students, I used the YMCA model as a warm-up, and I took my time explaining it.

The reason for taking my time was simple. I could teach all day long, but if no one was astute enough, humble enough, skilled enough, or motivated enough to learn, then my teaching would most likely be ineffective. It would be like "casting pearls before swine." So I made an effort to enlist the students as human beings first, and then as students. Here again, I took the opportunity to share my experience with them. I explained to the students how I used to be exactly like them, and how I would allow my ego to get me into all sorts of situations that could have been easily avoided. I told them how I got sent to juvenile hall in the ninth grade for pulling a knife on someone in class. I told them how I was stabbed by another kid because of my ego. I told them about the string of burglaries I pulled, one of which occurred at my own high school cafeteria. I often used, as an example of my arrogance, a race that I had in college. My ego was so charged that I thought I was faster than the speed of sound until a few guys showed me that I was an average runner at best. I went on to tell the students that, like them, I would attempt to make excuses for my failures instead of accepting them and using them to build a stronger foundation. Finally, I explained how I overcame my arrogance by simply asking myself the spiritual question—why?

In our society, we have taught students to play offense. We have taught them to ask why, but only in an arrogant, interrogational way, not as a humble self-inquiry. So instead of asking inward spiritual or character-driven questions ("Why would I disrupt the teacher's lesson and deprive my fellow students of an education?" or "Why would I break into my own school?" or "Why would I destroy my own body with drugs?"), students nowadays are more inclined to assign blame and ask external, offense-oriented questions ("Why are we doing this boring stuff?" or "Why are you giving me detention?" or "Why are these police such 'haters'?") In other words, they don't have the internal, intrinsic moral compass or the conscientious ability to think beyond their own interests. When urban underperforming students are taught to implement and use the self-reflective **why**—and I've seen it done—the students change completely.

I've had several opportunities to talk with students who changed after being taught about the third entity. When asked why they don't get involved in the dumb skirmishes any more, they often answer by saying that they simply don't have time for it. That's where we want them to be: conscious of their time.

On the next page is an example of the type of chart that I use to illustrate the tripartition of the human being. Also included in the chart is the essence of the human being—time, talent, and treasures (the 3Ts). This is all a person can acquire as a human being. This tripartition will be discussed in detail in the next section.

The Human Being

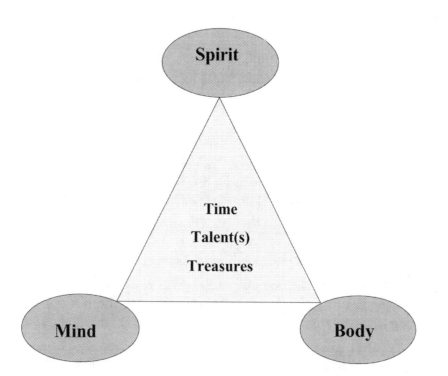

In closing, in the past, this humbling or humanizing process of development was accomplished in urban schools by teachers and administrators who had a vested interest in the students through a common experience. Unfortunately, for the most part, this dynamic no longer exists. Currently, everything revolves around academic subject matter. Therefore, it is essential that students in underperforming schools be placed in situations where they can truly get in touch with themselves fully. Minority people have been paying a tremendous price for the past twenty or thirty years because they have been deprived of this crucial knowledge. It may be profitable for students in more affluent environments to be separated from their traditional source of stability; however, the urban underperformer cannot afford to operate at such a deficit. We must restore the traditional tripartition of humanity in order to forge lasting positive relationships.

The 3Ts

As I mentioned earlier, it is absolutely clear to me that urban underperforming students are attempting to function as normal human beings while employing only two-thirds of what makes them human—mind and body. I see it on a daily basis. Their minds, via the ego, pump up their false esteem, and they end up in situations where their bodies must be put on the line in an attempt to defend the madness. Naturally, I am an advocate of teaching them about the third element—the spirit.

Once the students have been exposed to their threefold nature, the next step is to explain to them exactly what they gain by embracing themselves as full human beings. When students accept their humanity, the next step is for them to grasp that they immediately become the possessor and controller of three entities—their time, talents, and treasures.

We often tell students to stop wasting their time. But we rarely take the time to explain why. It is vital that students consciously realize the impact and control of *time* as a key component in their lives. This time factor also assists in establishing a sense of urgency, which is currently lacking. Therefore, when I talk with students about time, I use myself as an example. I tell them that if we follow the natural order of things, I will probably die before they do. I stress how one morning I woke up, looked in the mirror, and saw a gray beard, but I didn't feel distressed because I got out of my ignorant phase in time to create a decent life for myself. Don't worry about them understanding you, because if you have been developing a relationship with them, they will understand you fully and believe you.

Many kids in urban areas have bought, or been misdirected into, the belief that they should not pursue seriousness. Some parents, teachers, counselors, and especially the media constantly admonish them to have fun while they're young. This may be correct for some environments, but I think it's the wrong signal to send to urban underperforming students. Having fun for them might mean participating in detrimental behaviors: sex, drugs, gangs, crime, and violence. If these activities dominate the students' time, they often become more proficient in the conduct but drift further and further off the path of academic pursuits. And if there is no one to correct the behavior, as is often the case, the students never recover from the huge waste of time.

After helping the students gain control of their time, the next step is to get them focused on *talent* development. I tell them that each and every one of them has a talent that he is better at than anyone else in the room. I then tell them that their job is to find out what that talent is. By the time we get to this point, relationships have been forged and a mutual comfort zone established. I then inevitably get asked the question of how they determine their talents. My stock answer to them is this: "You have to get out there and try different things; whether it is sports, music, academics, or a host of other alternatives, you find out by being interested and participating."

Another thing that I try to teach students is how to recognize a true talent. I tell them that one way to know they are pursuing a real talent is by the amount of time that must be invested. Talent development takes time. I joke with the long shots and tell them, even though they may think differently, smoking marijuana is not a talent. I explain that pot smoking is something that I could teach their little brother to do in five or ten minutes. Therefore, because of the short learning curve, it doesn't qualify. I use reading as an example of a true talent. After all, it's something that begins in kindergarten and is not really perfected until college. Playing a musical instrument is another great example. But regardless of the example used, the point is that each student has a talent that must be developed in order to maximize his or her potential, and it takes a lot of time to accomplish it.

The last of the 3Ts is *treasures*, which are the natural result of spending your time developing talents. The only thing I try to do with the treasures component is stress that treasures are more than monetary. Through a series of posters, discussions, and writing prompts, I attempt to teach the students about real treasures. I try to get them to understand that reading, writing, thinking, playing a musical instrument, recreation and leisure time, health, fitness, and a multitude of other fully developed talents are all treasures. Then I present them with the knowledge of the ultimate treasure—a good family. I make no bones about it. I assure them if they spend their time developing the necessary talents for building a good family, the treasure of having one will be theirs.

The Environment:

- Layout and Climate (community, district, school, and classroom)

- Rites, Rituals, and Jobs

- Cleanliness

- Student Work Displays

- Professionalism (teacher dress, student dress, creation of quality materials and copies)

Knowing and understanding the students is essential to the success of any urban underperforming school. However, this knowledge of the student is only a portion of the relationship-building process. Understanding, developing, and maintaining a positive physical environment is equally important.

The classroom environment must have structure and be conducive to learning. However, the classroom is only a microcosm of what I mean by the environment. The environment actually includes any and all levels of direct and indirect influence on the teacher-student relationship. Examples include the home, the community, the school district, the particular school site, and the individual classroom. The environment actually plays a major role in molding and shaping the student typology.

The environment should be observed, investigated, and evaluated based upon five entities. The environmental entities include the *layout and climate,* followed by *rites, rituals, and jobs; cleanliness; work displayed; and professionalism*. These entities form the basis of study for anyone wishing to examine the environment and work with urban students.

Many may think that getting familiar with the environment is too much of a challenge; however, it's not. Most of the evaluating can be accomplished in a non-threatening, anecdotal fashion simply by making mental notes about the homes, community, district, and so on. Some observational questions that you might ask yourself include: Is there a high instance of single-parent families? Is the community inundated with graffiti? Do the youth of the community congregate on the street unsupervised? Are there thriving businesses, other than liquor stores and gas mini-marts, in the area? Is the school district staff racially, ethnically, and, somewhat, economically reflective of its service constituency? Is my school site a combative, hostile, and violent place for teachers or a supportive, calm, and nurturing environment? Is the principal supportive of teachers? Is my union's relationship with the district one of collaboration and cooperation or aggression and hostility? Questions like these will assist you when formulating an understanding about the environment and creating and developing your own classroom atmosphere.

When it comes to the confines of your classroom, the general approach will not suffice. You must be a direct participant in its development. Otherwise, you don't stand a genuine chance of being successful. So to insure that you will at least have a fighting chance in your classroom environment, allow me to walk you through my approach to the observation and development of a learning community.

Layout and Climate (home, community, district, school, and classroom)

On countless occasions, I have heard teachers from urban underperforming schools make comments, in one form or another, about how it doesn't matter what the administration tells you to do, because when your classroom door closes you can do it your way. To a certain extent, I agree with those teachers, but usually for a different reason. Of course, I believe that in many instances public school administrators are limited in their knowledge about urban underperforming schools and students. They usually don't know who they are or where they are coming from. So it would stand to reason that they would know little about what they need. But on the other hand, I don't believe that teachers should work in isolation. The closed-door policy could prove detrimental as well. The obvious problem is that the teacher could be seriously off-course, impeding student progress. I believe that the environmental, relationship-building effort should be a truly collaborative process between teachers and administrators, starting with a professional assessment based upon data collected from the outside.

As strange as this might sound, I believe that much of the building of an environment that is conducive to learning starts outside of the classroom, and the farther outside the better. That is why each and every time that I began work at a different school, I made a habit of walking through the surrounding community. Crisscrossing the community is a good way to determine what the specific norms and values are for that area and a good way to collect tidbits to use in the development of your own environment. Oftentimes I used my prep period as my excursion time. (And even if I don't learn anything new, the walking is a great stress reducer and a way to drop a few pounds.)

While walking, come out of your comfort zone and talk with a few people. It's a great way to find out what types of students you might end up with. Also take in the sights, sounds, and smells of the community. Hopefully you'll learn enough about what the people value to not make too many ignorant, ethnocentric faux pas. For instance, if you had walked through Mechanicsville, the neighborhood that I lived in as a child, you could have made several distinct observations. There were abandoned cars, dilapidated houses, yards with very little grass, and vacant lots with debris strewn about. Further examination would have revealed staggering drunks and a host of school-aged people wandering aimlessly. The sights would naturally be accompanied by the sounds of loud, boisterous, profane, sentence-fragmented discussions. And finally, there would be all of the smells that accompany poverty: odors like urine, the cooking of pinto beans, collards, cornbread, chitlins, beer, and cheap wine were the norm. In light of this, it would be somewhat inappropriate to talk too much about life in your beach house and the caviar, lobster, or escargot that you indulged in for dinner. Try to stifle your reality momentarily and live in theirs.

Home visits can also be an eye-opener. Many of my experiences include sitting on a dirty, roach-infested couch in a sunless room that smelled like a mixture of recently-smoked marijuana and other putrid organisms, drinking ice water that tasted like every single ingredient from the refrigerator, while being distracted by the television that was turned down, but not off, as a sign of respect. Then, there's the other side of home visits. At the homes of some of the community straight shots, you might actually be surprised to find out everything is normal by your standards. Then you've got something else to ponder.

Some of you are thinking, "He's crazy! I'm not going out there." Don't worry, you'll do just fine. In the vast majority of underperforming communities, even the hardcore ones, the community members actually respect teachers. Also, in many cases, they use the casual conversation they have with you as something of a status symbol with their friends. So don't fret the walk or the talk. But if you are still feeling apprehensive, take another teacher with you.

Far more important than the fear of walking the neighborhood is the question of what to do with the information that you garner. Start using it right away. This new knowledge will help you to better understand the students. It will also eliminate some of the shock value when the kids arrive mimicking the streets and trying to force a spill-over of street behavior into your classroom. As dean of students in a school that had a reputation for being hardcore (I thought it was a cakewalk), I had a young, first-year teacher from India come to me under some distress, saying, "Today was the first time that I have been called a bitch to my face." I immediately diagnosed the problem as a relationship deficiency. It wasn't that she had never heard the word before. I'm sure that she'd been to the movies. The problem was that she had not desensitized herself to the environment. This mild version of culture shock could have been avoided if she had walked from the school to the park, which was less than one block away, and simply observed the interactions between the people. She would have heard that word being used in such a casual fashion by little gangster wannabes, and if she preferred to see it in print, "bitch" and worse was written all over the restroom walls, park benches, and adjacent street signs. In this instance, the issue should not have been what the student said, but what the teacher's response was after the statement.

Another valuable reason for walking through the neighborhood is the collection of names for dropping later. When you meet these community members while out walking, it would be great if you actually attempted to forge a relationship with them; but if that's too much in the beginning, just get some of their names and don't be afraid to drop them in class. Tell the students about some of the people you met and the conversations you had with them. Somehow weave them into the lesson. Chances are some of your students will know some of them too.

During the 2004 to 2005 school year, I was out walking in the neighborhood and ran across a couple of young teenagers who appeared to be truant. I told them who I was and asked why they weren't in school. The group spokesman told me that he already knew who I was, and that they were middle-school students running late. The student was probably being something less than honest about their status, but what I took away from the encounter was this: even though I worked at the high school, the word was already out, and the middle-school long shots had already received it. For the students to know who I was meant that relationship building was well on the way. So take a short hike.

Along with checking out the community, you should also be checking out your district, your union, and your school site. You need to know how each of these entities functions, but don't get involved in too many of the minute details about the district and the union. They have a way of monopolizing a lot of your time. So unless you are deliberately pursuing a career in one or the other, don't show too much interest. You can easily be drawn into countless hours of often thankless, *pro bono* work.

If your district administration is knowledgeable and supportive of their schools and their teachers, then you have found Shangri-La. But if they aren't supportive, you'll know that too. In most cases, if you have landed in a non-supportive environment, your district and school site will have an anti-teacher air and you will feel like the sacrificial lamb all the time. Furthermore, there will be an ongoing game of "train and blame" being played out. The district and the school sites will spend their time creating a host of different training programs that have virtually nothing to do with the problems at your school, followed by running the teachers through a barrage of workshops. Upon completion, they test the students. When the students' academic performance doesn't improve, the administration blames the teachers for not embracing and implementing their unrelated, ineffective programs properly. Then the whole cycle begins again with a new series of even less relevant programs.

If your intuition is totally impaired and you fail to get it, don't fret, because your union (association) representatives should tell you what's going on. Another slight caveat about unions is in order. Under ideal circumstance, unions shouldn't be necessary; however, in many districts, conditions are radically less than ideal. This less-than-ideal situation makes unions not only necessary but practically essential. Unions, like the district, normally promote and support a one-sided point of view. In the case of the union, it's the best interest of its members—primarily teachers. Unions generally pursue what they perceive as equitable and fair treatment of their members, but sometimes they can be extremely political and self-serving in the process. I am, and will continue to be, fairly active in my union as long as I am in education because it's currently a necessary service. However, I wish that districts and unions could get on the same page. It would be better for the students. With that said, I encourage you to investigate and support your union because, after all, this is your chosen profession and the source of your livelihood. But never forget that this entire endeavor is about the education of students. With a general understanding of the outside layout and climate, you are now ready to work on developing your classroom environment.

It is imperative that you have a plan in mind for the layout and structuring of your classroom. The only advice that I will offer is this. Don't design your classroom to look like the neighborhood or local community environment, and don't leave the environment to chance. If you design it to resemble the neighborhood, or if you fail to design it at all, the students will establish the structure. When they determine the configuration, you can expect to see the same things in your environment as in theirs, and you can expect the same things that happen in their environment to happen in your classroom—profanity, sordid conversations, posing and posturing, arguments, fights, tagging, graffiti, and a host of other trifling activities. I'll boast a bit here. In nine-plus years of working in "difficult" environments—a prison boot camp, as well as zero-tolerance and alternative-atypical schools—I've had zero fights in my classes. I believe the relative calm can be directly attributed to the environmental structure and my willingness to stand up to maintain its composition. I try to make the environment teacher-student, but not *long-shot* friendly. I accomplish this in part by implementing ***rites, rituals and jobs, cleanliness, student work displays, and professionalism.***

Rites, Rituals, and Jobs

Rites, rituals, and jobs are the three pillars for building a classroom climate that is conducive to learning. They also go a long way towards the establishment of you—the teacher—as the ultimate leader of the class while demonstrating your desire to invite the students to participate. Although I was implementing this theory as part of routine classroom practices, I discovered that author Ralph Peterson, in his book *Life in a Crowded Place* (1992), had already assigned labels describing this trio. So, I pilfered his terminology. Rites, rituals, and jobs assist by setting a tone for behavior, creating responsibility, and encouraging team building. In short, they build relationships.

Rites are momentary pauses to recognize student achievements, task mastery, or milestones. To insure that they don't become pauses to hang targets on the backs of the straight shots, rites should be created that have meaning but can be achieved virtually by all. Rites are designed to serve two purposes—intrinsic reward and extrinsic motivation. **Rituals** are the norms and mores of an environment, but with greater specificity. They are to be practiced on a daily basis. I use things like greetings, handshakes, and titles. I also ritualistically follow a schedule of daily events, and if I don't follow it on a given day for some reason or another, I make a huge deal about the deviation, and then I get back on track the very next day. This creates a sense of true stability and gives an added boost to the importance and urgency of our mission—

creating treasure. It's the time-talent development thing. Lastly, create jobs. I create tons of them. I have so many jobs in my class that I even make a job out of keeping track of who has which job; I call that person the class scribe. **Jobs** can include book distributor and inspector (this is a great job for long shots; it gives them responsibility and keeps down the tagging), the official readers (coveted by the straights, and they keep me from becoming hoarse), the video equipment specialist (who sets up the equipment, clicks through PowerPoint presentations, turns overheads, sets up the television for videos and DVDs), the organization expert (insures that all notebooks and magazines are collected and placed into proper baskets or files, colored pencils are boxed and stored away, extra handouts are collected and filed, and so on). There's the cleanup woman, man, or crew, who check for trash and make sure all of the chairs are pushed under the desks, or placed atop them if the custodian will be cleaning on that day. They also erase the whiteboard and write the next day's lesson on the board. And, lastly, I always assign someone the job of timer. This individual keeps us on pace to complete the day's assignments, which also reiterates the urgency aspect of our mission. The more jobs you come up with, the greater the buy-in and less turmoil at the end of each class.

In the classroom, it is vital that real unity be present. Unity is one of the major forces in the development of any stable environment. Unity is the glue that binds families together and propels them in the direction of whatever their goal might be. And nothing builds unity like rites, rituals, and jobs.

On a daily basis, as a teacher, I would offer a genuine greeting to each and every student as they entered my classroom, and when the period was over, bid them a warm, culturally-significant farewell. These gestures or pleasantries were a form of ritualistic behavior, but I would go a step further. If it was a Friday, I'd be sure to jokingly tell the kids something like "Be careful shoplifting this weekend," or "Have a great weekend, and make sure that you are in bed by seven-thirty." Then on Monday, as a way of bolstering our relational connection, I'd ask someone to talk openly about something they did over the weekend. If appropriate, I would try to tie the comments to something dealing with history. But if the comment is of a sensitive nature, sometimes it's better to pause in recognition of the incident, give a foreboding sigh, and move on. When the students start to initiate the Monday dialogue, you know that you've made relational progress.

I would also often shake the student's hand and add the title of "sir," "ma'am," "young lady," "young man," "brother," "sister," "barrister," or even "doctor" to their names as they entered the classroom. Of course, from time to time, a long shot couldn't resist the temptation and would ask me why I called them "sir" or "doctor," and that's what I lived for. I would make a party out of the question and sometimes take as long as five minutes to answer. It was a great time to make it known that a long shot had the capacity to ask a curious and insightful question. (This acknowledgement of the long shot's potential is also an effective strategy to win him over.) Further, if I answered to the long shot's satisfaction (meaning that he has no wiggle room to make a logically cutting comeback), I could directly influence the sling shots. By the way, my patented response was this: the titles were my aspiration for them. (The word "aspiration" might need explaining, but I use the word anyway as a vocabulary builder.) I would then follow up by saying it was up to them to realize and fulfill that aspiration.

Another point I want to introduce here, even though it might be as much a part of the section dealing with the teacher, is how the students address you. In my opinion, one of the worst possible things that teachers in urban underperforming schools can do is allow the students to address them using their first names in or outside of the environment. Addressing you as Mr., Mrs., or Ms. is a huge ritual itself and a major part of your leadership persona, even if you're only twenty-two years old. The less formal approach may work in higher-performing environments, where the competition for respect might be less prevalent, but in urban underperforming school environments, respect—real or perceived—is everything. The use of the title is a huge form of respect. Several years back, I worked with a first-year counselor at a zero-tolerance school. Prior to her contact with the students, we talked about the issue of formal titles. She was adamant about having the students call her by her first name or, if pressed, by her first name with Ms. added. I cautioned against it. After that first year, we revisited the issue. To her credit, after calculating the cost in terms of the constant challenges to her authority, she realized that the informal approach was not the proper course, and reversed strategy. I still talk with her from time to time, and things are going great. A little extra added superlative like Mr. or Ms. might make all the difference.

Other ritualistic acts are the posting and walking through of the daily scheduled activities and the Monday morning briefing, which serve as general reminders of the classroom rules and regulations. By the way, don't become angry when they begin to openly mock you while you are reciting and repeating the rules; that means that they got it. If anything, it's time for you to make the task into a job. Rites and rituals are magnificent relationship builders, but jobs are indispensable. Whether in a classroom or greater society, work builds dignity and self-esteem. Incorporate this trinity into your class environment.

Cleanliness

The level of cleanliness is often the student's way of measuring how you feel about what you are doing. Therefore, cracking down on cleanliness is vital. Allow me to approach this from another perspective. Deep down inside, long and sling shots admire the straight shots, but they don't usually pursue their ranks for fear of being intellectually rebuffed. Why do they admire them? They can recognize the comparative positive difference. Because they are long shots, don't think that they cannot recognize and identify quality; they can. It's the same way with cleanliness in the class environment. Deep down inside, the longs and slings respect and desire it, but they don't want to run the risk of being reproved for putting forth the effort to claim it. It's like the respect offered to churches. Students will bypass three churches on their way to graffiti the school. Why? It's because most students recognize what is understood to be sacred.

If you can build an environment and treat it with something akin to veneration and distinction, the students will generally treat it the same way. This effort will go a long way towards eliminating turf disputes and other disruptions as well. If the environment doesn't remotely resemble their turf—the neighborhood streets—and if it's already made clear whose turf it is—yours, then that will normally clear up any disputes. When I was in the classroom, I would go to any length to remove every single tag (gang insignia) from the walls, furniture, floor, and ceiling prior to any student setting foot inside. I was such a stickler about this that I even checked the door jambs inside and out. (By the way, graffiti patrolman is a great job for hardcore reforming long shots. They won't be afraid of the consequences from the other long shots for detecting and removing them, and the other students will respect them enough not to deface their work.)

Some might think that it isn't necessary to discuss the importance of maintaining a clean classroom environment, but I think that it's not only important but paramount. When I speak of cleanliness, I mean more than simply sweeping the floor. What I mean is everything from garbage to gum to graffiti. Everyone has heard the saying that cleanliness is next to godliness. I happen to believe that is true, especially in urban underperforming schools. After more than nine years of investigative observation and implementation, I can attest and explain why a clean environment is a vital piece of the urban educational puzzle. The level of cleanliness is a method by which teachers can determine whether the environment is theirs or not. Further, cleanliness in your environment is to be used like the ghetto safe-house code—"Respect my Crib." In my old neighborhood, my crew and I could trash the streets together, but we were obliged to respect each other's homes. In effect, the level of cleanliness is a mood barometer. It is also your offering to the students as a safe and inviting cocoon. When I taught at the zero-tolerance school, at lunchtime, many students would bring their lunches to my room and eat. They'd talk, play chess and other games, and then clean up the place and leave. They didn't necessarily go there because they liked me; they went because they knew that the environment was going to be clean and safe.

On numerous occasions I have heard teachers, even veteran ones, say they don't care how the room looks. They believe there are larger issues to be dealt with: fighting, disrespect, and, when the opportunity presents itself, teaching. What they fail to see is that fighting is potentially a by-product of the lack of respect derived from the level of cleanliness observed. Fights do occur at urban underperforming schools, but they usually do not take place in the environments that are respected areas. So, keep your place tidy. Sweep, vacuum, wipe off the desk, and clean the windows. If you're thinking that's the custodian's job, you are right; it is. However, the custodian isn't necessarily trying to create a learning community. You are! If the custodian is not doing his job, you can hound him about it or take the matter to your principal. If the complaint falls on deaf ears, I suggest that you clean the room yourself; afterwards, you can make a student job out of it. If your area is not clean, the students will not be sympathetic. Students need to know and understand what you value, not what the custodian doesn't; that's the principal's job.

Lastly, keep yourself clean and well-groomed. This issue will be discussed further in the subsection on professionalism and again in the section on the teacher. But for now, just understand that when you are groomed and clean, it completes the picture. There is no contradiction in the message.

Student Work Displays

Display quality work from past and present students. Displaying work from students over a period of years allows current students to feel as though they are part of something out of the ordinary. I also talk about the former students who created and produced the work whenever the opportunity presents itself. Another reason to display work is this: it sets a high standard and it gives the students a vital look at what the standard of excellence is for the class. Without you expressing it to them verbally, your students will sense the expectation and the possibilities. They will naturally explore the possibility of their own academic immortality. They will actually think about the fact that someday it might be them and their work that you stand and speak of after they have moved on. Using this strategy, I have had students get so caught up in the possibility of being immortalized that they will secretly come to me and ask if I believe their work will meet the standard of the immortals, and if not, to seek advice for improvement. I have also had ex-students return to see if their work was still being used as a display model. When the bar for quality is placed before the students and set high, they work harder, buy into the academic focus more readily, and work to become part of a culture of achievement.

Professionalism (teacher attire, student attire, development of quality materials and copies)

Professionalism is exceedingly critical. Treat the students and the environment with a high degree of professionalism, and it becomes contagious. You are the most important part of the professional standard. Dress and groom at a high level of professionalism, and the students will respond with a high degree of professionalism. I believe this so deeply that whenever I am on the school grounds, unless participating in a special event that requires less, I wear a freshly-pressed shirt and a tie. I also make sure that my pants are creased and my shoes shined. Periodically, students will ask me why I dress up every day, and that's my teachable moment. I tell them that an old football coach once told me that if I intended to be the best player on the team, I had to practice like I intended to play the game. In other words, treat every day as though it were game day. Teaching was the new game I was playing, and I intended to come ready to play every day. Also, because the students are usually extremely price-conscious, I use it as a way to dispel some of their distorted economic myths. With all of the misguided information permeating their minds about brand names and the stigma of being labeled as cheap, I could easily use the cost of clothing and leap-frog right into history, government, and, of course, economics. I make certain that I never miss an opportunity to discuss cost. I explain how even though I dress professionally, it doesn't mean that I'm buying expensive clothing. I point out that most of my ties are bought on clearance from stores like J.C. Penney and how, in many cases, I paid as little as $1.77 for each of them. They usually laugh—that is until I leap-frog to the subject of investing the savings in stocks, bonds, and mutual funds. Then they usually get it.

Along those same lines, I also demand that students dress appropriately. If the school has a dress code, I enforce it. I did it as a teacher, and I certainly do it as dean of students. As dean, to drive home the message of professionalism via appropriate dress, I would stand in front of the school each and every morning and pull out the students who didn't meet the dress code standard. I wouldn't then, and won't ever, tolerate exposed bellies and backs, saggy pants, or inappropriate messages printed on clothing. When a student violates the code there are two options—change into apparel we provide or call home for a change. Also, just as a side note, I don't believe in the practice of school uniforms. This strategy may work in parochial schools, where they reinforce the behavior with other proselytizing rituals. However, in urban underperforming schools, it may simply be treated as a precursor of, and conditioning for, the institutional uniforms to come. I'd rather see students learn to wear their own clothes appropriately. This strategy works best when all staff members present a united front.

The next professional thing I try to do is provide clear-cut instructions. Clear instructions are a component of professionalism, and so is the distribution of high-quality handouts. When providing instructions, if necessary, issue them in all three lingoes: long, sling, and straight. When distributing handouts, make certain that the printer you use is reproducing high-quality copies. When it isn't, demand better. I'm such a stickler when it comes to copy quality that I would rather not issue a copy at all than hand out one with shadows and copy burns on it. I think it's a poor reflection of your professionalism when you distribute junk. The students may not say anything, but they notice it. Along those same lines, if you are willing to challenge yourself to be professional, you should also challenge your students to be the same. I always issue a simple reminder. I tell them to remember that they are not producing work for themselves but for me to read, judge, and score. Then I inform them that if I can't read it, I will not score it. I also tell them up front that I will not score papers that are written in Old English, or with gang stylized writing, and neither will I accept drawings in the margins or tattered edges torn from notebooks. And I stand firm. After all, after nine or ten years of attending school, students already have a sense of quality. So in many cases, when they turn in soiled, low-quality, graffiti-riddled work, it isn't done because they don't know better; it's done as a way of testing your tolerance and professionalism, and ultimately to determine if you can and will check the unruliness.

One final point on professionalism: don't become the students' source for school supplies. You might think that you are helping that poor kid who couldn't afford supplies. It doesn't help them or you. When a student is constantly coming to you for supplies, two negative things are usually transpiring. First, it might be another test. Second, if it's not about game playing, you may be enabling the student through this type of philanthropic behavior.

When I worked at a middle school site for zero-tolerance students, there was a teacher assigned there who had transferred to our district from Saint Louis, Missouri, with more than fifteen years of teaching experience. One day, she showed up for work with her arms filled with of all kinds of treats and snacks. She had everything from caramel corn to miniature candy bars. When I asked what was going on, she said that she was going to use them as rewards to promote positive behavior. She then told me that based upon previous conversations, she knew I would disapprove. And she was right; I did indeed disapprove. And within two weeks of the implementation of her positive reinforcement program, it also became clear to her that it was a bad initiative.

Back then, during my prep period, I often left campus to take a walk. One day, as I returned from walking, the teacher met me at the front door with that "something happened while you were gone" look on her face. She said that while I was out, someone had stolen a fairly large sum of money from her purse. I already knew who to focus on to pinpoint the culprit.

When I was leaving the building, I had walked past her room and seen several members of her positive reinforcement program munching on snacks, bouncing off the walls, and wheeling around the room in her desk chair. After getting the counselor to cover my classroom for the period, I went into her office and began calling the students that I saw in the teacher's room, one by one. Within a half-hour, I knew who had taken the money. Within an hour, we had the money back. When I asked the student why he had taken the money, he said that she was always giving them stuff, and he wanted to see if he could get away with it. In other words, he thought that she was already their trick, and he wanted to see just how deep into the game she was. If she had let the incident slide, they would have taken it as a green light to do whatever they wanted to her. After that, she promised to stop with the treats.

So whether you are enabling or encouraging low-level scheming, both are potentially destructive. Don't reward students for doing something that is its own intrinsic reward: learning. When students ask me for supplies, I usually respond by asking, "Do I look like the welfare office?" I then tell them they can borrow from a friend or I will sell them the item, because I don't want them to get used to accepting handouts. (I'm also the same way when it comes to giving answers to questions and providing definitions of vocabulary words. That's stuff they could easily research for themselves. I give them the tools to do it.) And if students do happen to purchase a pencil from me, it comes with a long lecture about the power of one pencil to change their life. At the end of the speech, I go on to inform them that if they bring the same pencil back to me at the end of the semester I will refund their purchase price. A few have actually taken me up on it. And one kid that I had taught in middle school several years earlier, who ended up at the high school where I was dean, came by my office one day just to recite my pencil lecture to me. He never forgot it. (Note that many districts do not tolerate the selling of supplies to students.) Make the students responsible for being professionals—no pardons and no excuses.

Discipline:

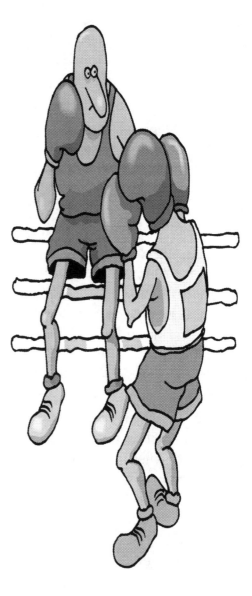

- ✓ What is discipline?
- ✓ Why discipline?
- ✓ District/School Discipline Plan
- ✓ Your Philosophy and Plan
- ✓ TSMP model
- ✓ Conflict (the Chinese model)

What is discipline?

According to the Collaborative International Dictionary of English, discipline is defined as "the treatment suited to a disciple or learner [or student]; education; development of the faculties by instruction and exercise; training, whether physical, mental, or moral."

In order to achieve this discipline, I believe that a closer examination of its components is necessary. As I see it, discipline contains three components: ***control, denial,*** and ***focus***. It is the mastery of these components that will lead to full discipline and, thus, the maximum mental, physical, and moral opportunity to achieve positive and proper instruction and training. In the urban public, underperforming school environment, the mastery of discipline is imperative.

In order to be disciplined, students must first be able to control themselves. That is, they must become accountable to themselves for the monitoring of their own behavior, although, in many cases, they have no desire or incentive to do so. I place this responsibility squarely on the shoulders of the students even though the latest rhetoric bashes anyone who does this. They call it blaming the victim; I say it's making individuals accountable for their behavior. Why do I say this? Because even if parents don't teach or demand self-control from their children, by the time students reach middle or high school, they have seen plenty of examples of what it looks like and the proper situational response. In essence, they already know how to control themselves, if they want to. Therefore, in the majority of cases, the lack of control is actually a selective process rather than an issue of incapacity. But many school officials and counselors create and foster the victim mentality by treating this selective process as though it is a social or biological incapacity problem. When this is done, behaviors that could be easily rectified often end up being assigned labels like "oppositional defiance," "attention deficit disorder," or "emotionally disturbed." These types of excuses often encourage more negative behavior. And, even worse, in some cases, counselors, psychologists, and administrators have released the students from responsibility altogether by placing blame on the teachers for their inability to meaningfully engage the students. Are there ever situations where a student has a genuine mental disorder? Yes! However, in urban underperforming schools, there appear to be too many diagnoses based on a lack of self-control. Under these circumstances, the students have absolutely no incentive to change their behavior. We are not only creating an environment that is not conducive to learning, but we are potentially destroying the lives and futures of these young people by allowing them to leave school believing that they have an excuse or are somehow exempt from being responsible for managing their behavior.

When urban underperforming students leave school, society is going to demand self-control from them for the rest of their lives. If they fail to demonstrate appropriate management skills, it is going to cost them dearly. This lack of control could cost them socially and economically. And if we examine the current trends, it might even cost them their freedom via incarceration. We have to buck this trend. So, what should we do as school personnel to counteract this control problem? For starters, if individual students don't or won't manage themselves, teachers and the administrative staff must step in and fill the void without being so quick to paint the students as victims.

In urban underperforming school settings, when it comes to the control component, I have observed a great deal of buck-passing. The excuse for not dealing with the issue is the fear of doing greater harm to the alleged victim. However, in reality, it appears to be actual fear of the alleged victim that results in the failure to intervene. The bottom line is that you cannot be afraid of the students. If it comes down to the adults controlling the situation, they must be disciplined enough to do it without fear and without feeling bad about the enforcement. They must view the correction as a necessary process designed to better the student's life, not just in the present circumstance, but beyond.

In order to forge control, the first thing I suggest a teacher or staff member do is determine if the underperforming school is the right setting for you to practice your profession. Assuming you conclude that it is, I then suggest that you develop and promote strategies to support and enforce self-control on your campus for the students and the staff. For my classroom, I created a poster program using discipline components—control, denial, and focus—as writing and discussion prompts. I also used a medley of other strategies, some of which will be discussed later in this section.

After gaining control via internal or external means, students must then learn self-denial. Students must learn to reject juvenile thoughts and renounce and turn down the temptation to pursue trifling immediate gratification. As with control, in most cases students have already sufficiently developed the mechanism for self-denial. They already know that there is a time and place for all things. In urban underperforming schools, the students simply need to be persuaded to accept their school as a venue where immature pleasures and spontaneous outbursts are tempered. It is at this juncture that the school staff becomes pivotal.

As leaders of the learning environment, teachers and administrators must be committed to insuring that students believe in the educational course of action at their school so strongly that they will readily employ and monitor their own denial system. If by chance there are a few students who need to learn how to suppress desires, there must be a program in place to promptly confront, control, resolve, and redirect the students. This program, of course, must start with leadership. Teachers, staff, and administrators must display self-denial as well. Certain indulgences, like being late and not being prepared with relevant, challenging and thought-provoking lessons, or being afraid to step outside of your comfort zone to challenge students who are creating discipline problems, must be renounced. One of the most serious threats to the learning environment in underperforming schools that I have witnessed is adult apathy: When adults see students doing something that is a clear violation of policies and procedures, and totally detrimental to themselves and the school culture, but do nothing to correct the behavior. The students aren't stupid. When the adults will not deny themselves and emerge from their comfort zone to confront infractions, why should students deny themselves their juvenile urges? So, as teachers, staff and administrators, denial, unlike control, starts with you.

The third component of discipline is focus. Focus is fairly complex. Focus is the ingredient needed for direction and talent development. However, unless it is given as a mandate at home, most students really don't know how to choose one. As with denial, teachers, staff members, and administrators factor heavily into the equation. Urban underperforming staffs must be armed with a lucid, intelligible, big-picture focus that can readily be explained and translated into a personal, embraceable focus for individual students. If the school does not have a focus, expect the long shots to be waiting in the wings with theirs. And to a great extent, that's exactly what I think is occurring in many underperforming settings: the long shots are creating the school's focus.

In order to combat this focus deficiency, I would recommend that underperforming schools have a focus plan in writing. Your plan should, at the very least, include your philosophy of education, your goal and strategy for student achievement, and a discipline plan. I suggest that the plan be reviewed and modified as often as necessary to insure its effectiveness. I further suggest that posters be created to convey the concept of discipline which includes focus. Also, develop writing warm-ups and other activities around the entire discipline theme. Following is a sample discipline poster:

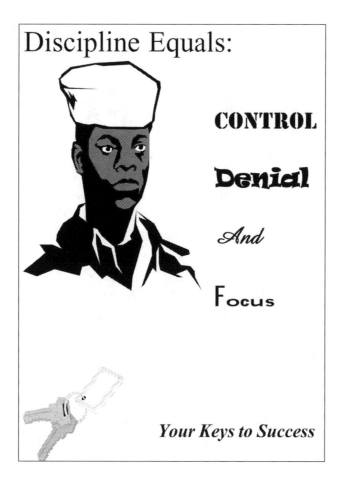

Lastly, whether in English, health, or another course, have students create their own focus plan. If they create a plan themselves, they won't be aimlessly wondering and waiting for some harebrained long shot to offer his version. The plan should include a statement of where they are, where they want to go, and the process for getting there. If possible, place a copy in the student's permanent record and allow them to revisit and modify it over time.

As a final suggestion, try not to get into the habit of rewarding the urban underperforming students for demonstrating good discipline. It's something that they already know they should be employing. Besides, as they progress, they'll recognize the achievement, and their esteem will rise in a more natural way.

Why discipline?

Discipline is necessary for two reasons: safety and to facilitate learning. Regardless of the activity or environment, if the location is not safe and if the populace doesn't feel at ease, the event will operate at less than its maximum positive capacity. This notion of safety is so central to human performance that it led the American psychologist Abraham Maslow to list safety and security as the second of his six levels to be attained on the path to self-actualization, or the fulfillment of the human potential.

Only physiological needs, such as food, shelter, and clothing, ranked higher. Safety needs ranked ahead of the need for love, belonging, and academic strategies.

Students who feel threatened or unsafe are far more likely to spend their time attempting to procure a sense of well-being. Above the building of relationships and the completion of abstract class assignments is the search for a sense of well-being, and the problem with students attempting to secure their own safety and security is obvious. Their idea of procuring safety normally includes all of the things that lead to instability and even greater anxiety—actions like carrying a concealed weapon, claiming gang affiliation, false bravado, and excessive humor and horseplay. All of these impede learning. On the other hand, students who feel secure and relieved of this burden are more inclined to be relaxed and directly open to the educational process.

In order to create a feeling of relative safety, one of the first things I would do in my introduction to my class was to put my reputation on the line. I did this by guaranteeing the students that they would be safe because I would defend and protect them. I promised them I would handle the knuckleheads (long shots), and I encouraged them to trust me. I then went a step further and asked them to relax and concentrate on being a regular student for a change. My final offering to them was more of a warning. I told them that if they attempted to take matters into their own hands without first giving me a shot at resolving the problem, I would come down hard on them, right along with all of the other administrative authorities.

After giving this protective homily, I would see some of the most disruptive, gangster-acting students appear to instantly calm down. Some even came to me after class to ask for assistance in getting a rival off their back. This approach confirmed a point that I had long presumed: the only reason many of the students—longs and slings—misbehave is to present a macho persona as a method of warding off potential antagonists. A student coming to ask for help is exactly what you want to have happen, but that's actually when the real work starts.

In order to make a grandiose promise to check the drama, you have to mean it. That's where the full support and leadership of your principal comes into play. If your administrator will not back you up, get out of that school fast. Fortunately for me, in all but one of my work sites, after explaining my entire program to the principal, for the most part, I've been supported.

After safety, the reason for discipline is to facilitate learning. Chaos is an environment that only disseminates more chaos. Several years ago when I was a police officer, a Montessori school opened on my beat. I didn't know what Montessori schools were all about. I only knew that the facility was very small and in a fairly affluent neighborhood. Because I am naturally curious, I started an investigation into their academic paradigm.

I started the investigation process by asking the officer on the beat next to mine to tell me what he knew about the program. He told me that based on what he had picked up in conversations with others, Montessori was a system of teaching where the students got to do whatever they wanted, and they learned because they were the initiators of the discovery. I couldn't believe it. They were letting the students do whatever they wanted, and they were still learning. When I heard that, my immediate thought was that he had to be kidding. Then I thought that if they were really doing that, I hoped the system would never be sprung on any urban, poor, black kids. I could envision a trail of dead and dying students and teachers strewn throughout the school in a matter of days. I thought that surely there had to be more to it than my beat buddy had alleged, so I went to the next phase of my investigation—academic and scientific research. I found out that Maria Montessori, an Italian educator and physician, developed the system and introduced it in Rome in 1907 (Microsoft Encarta 2000). The curriculum did stress development through self-reliance, and it indeed allowed the students to select academic components that interested them. However, it wasn't done quite like my colleague had envisioned. Even though the students got to select things that interested them, it was all done under "strict" disciplinary guidelines and within "controlled limits." So learning was occurring; however, it was being accomplished by adhering to strict discipline guidelines. Discipline is absolutely necessary for the facilitation of learning.

District/School Discipline Plan

Even though, in many cases, it may be offered as showcasing and window-dressing, each and every school district is mandated by the state to have a written policy or plan for school safety and student discipline. For example, the California Board of Education requires each school district to have a policy statement on discipline. This statement must clearly define the unacceptable behaviors and prescribe consequences for violators. The statement should also include a section that distinguishes discipline problems from law enforcement problems (real crimes). Per the state, the discipline policy should provide details on the following:

- Rights and responsibilities of students

- District discipline philosophy and goals

- Specific offenses and logical consequences

- Description of disruptive behaviors that interfere with the classroom learning environment, such as anti-social behaviors, tardiness and excessive absences

- Student code of conduct

- Provisions for appeals, hearings, and grievances

Earlier, I called this showcasing and window-dressing, and the reason is this. All that the state asks districts to do is make a few statements and then offer some legalistic details pertaining to the policing of the program. There is absolutely nothing preventative in the mandate. My guess would be that the state officials are a bunch of straight shots attempting to do what they do best, create and design programs that sound logical on paper but are virtually useless on the ground.

Beyond the state directive, get familiar with your district and school site discipline plan, and then develop a plan of your own. For the most part, individual districts will usually make a general statement about discipline. Their goal is simply to comply with state requirements. Beyond that, the district will frequently handle the more serious violations that carry a consequence of possible expulsion. In my school district, the district office basically provides an outline for suspensions, expulsions, and zero tolerance offenses, and their consequences. They also provide a venue for the placement and appeals process for affected students, and campus police (for crimes only). All other generalized, written disciplinary policies are agreed upon, in a negotiated collective bargaining process, between the San Diego City School District and the San Diego Education Association. Embedded in the teachers' contract is a section that specifically addresses pupil discipline. For example, the contract clearly directs the principal, along with the staff and school governance team (a body consisting of parents, teachers, administrators, and community members) to develop a site-specific student discipline plan.

While writing this book, I was employed at Samuel Gompers High School in San Diego. This school had developed a fairly reasonable plan. It contained a set of strategies, interventions, and consequences. The Gompers plan instructed teachers to post the school rules in plain view for the students. The rules were drawn directly from the District's suspension/expulsion policy and included acts such as class disruption, defiance of authority, threats and extortion, fighting and challenges to fight, drug possession, vandalism, and so on. The plan is pretty extensive and even goes as far as providing teachers with a comprehensive format or process to follow for implementing the discipline plan. The consequences include a breakdown by offense. For the first offense, a warning is issued; the second requires a telephone call to the parent or guardian; third, detention with the teacher; fourth, double the detention and calling the parent for a second time; and the final step is a written referral to the vice-principal, dean, or counselor. There wasn't much of a difference in the suggested interventions for teachers to use to maintain classroom discipline. Some of the interventions included changing the student's seat, conferencing with the student, sending the student to a buddy teacher's room, lowering the student's citizenship grade, withholding privileges, calling the parent, and consulting with the counselor. (I personally felt that this was too cumbersome for the teachers. Further, it only identified the offenses and prescribed consequences. It offered no preventative measures. I eventually created a process that streamlined the plan while providing an opportunity for relationship-building.)

As one can see, when it comes to student discipline, no preemptive or preventative measures are being offered. Everybody is busy passing the buck. With a few statements, the state passes it to the school district. After pulling out the more serious offenses and creating an appeals process, the district passes it on to the union officials. Union negotiators insert more directives and then pass it on to the school site governance team. The governance team, which typically consists of persons loyal to the principal, passes it on to the principal. The principal forms a committee, which frequently consists of his or her inner circle, and they create a plan that diverts the responsibility away from them to the teachers. As unfair as it may seem, that's where the buck stops, with the teachers. Under normal circumstances, this would be okay. But if you are in an urban underperforming school, you better have a plan and implement it pronto.

Your Philosophy and Plan

Now that you know that the buck stops with the teacher, it is easy to see why teachers in urban underperforming schools must have a philosophy of education and a discipline plan. Unless you are working in a teacher-respected and teacher-friendly environment, when it comes to discipline, you really are on your own. Why? Because many of the leaders in urban underperforming schools are too busy scrambling to cover their own backs and trying to avoid the blame and accusations from their leadership to care about your plight. In fact, you are more likely to become a scapegoat for your leadership than a relationship-building partner in this instance. So within the parameters of your state and your district and school policy, come up with a plan. Start with a philosophy.

Develop an Educational Philosophy, and then Create an Individual Discipline Plan.

Prior to developing a discipline plan, you should determine your educational philosophy. After all, your discipline plan will be a natural extension of your philosophy. An educational philosophy is a generalized statement regarding your belief about education in general. It should contain, at a minimum, a clear and acceptable theoretical philosophy that you actually believe. Some established philosophies include progressivism, existentialism, behaviorism, and essentialism. If you find that your philosophy is incompatible with the established views, you may choose to leave that school, or you can try to advance your own separate and independent philosophical belief. However, this could create a problem in your district if your philosophy deviates or conflicts too much with their philosophy. My personal philosophy is something of a soft blending of my own, mostly conservative, thoughts and beliefs with John Dewey's instrumentalism (which is a variation of William James' pragmatism). I believe that everything, the education of students included, depends on adaptability to the circumstances. If the school is in an urban, poor area and has underperformed for an extended period, I would be of the belief that the problem ought to be dealt with from an urban-poor perspective and if at all possible by successful ex-urban underperformers. And if that is not possible, it should be dealt with by those who have been trained to deal with the social conditions first and the academic issue second. Currently, we are attempting to solve a low academic performance problem with an incompatible, non-relational solution—more academic training of the teachers.

After establishing an educational philosophy, you can then get down to the business of creating your discipline plan. Here, instead of discussing options, I will provide my approach to discipline. Feel free to use any, all, or none of it. I merely want to provide you with a working model.

I keep it simple. I develop my discipline plan out of my classroom rule—RESPECT. That's right. I develop my entire discipline plan around one rule. I demand it, and I'm relentless in the pursuit of it. After all, it's right, legal, and good, and it's something they already understand. Urban underperforming students usually come from an environment where respect is everything. They know and see people every day who are willing to live and die for respect. If they didn't understand what respect meant, most of them wouldn't make it to school each day without being killed. So, by the time they are in high school, they know how to walk the respect tightrope. The issue is not whether or not they understand the rule, but whether they respect you enough to adhere to your benchmark of respect.

My standards are as follows: respect staff, fellows, and the environment. I demand respect in these three areas which, in reality, include everything. I also produce an extra-large poster version (like the one on the next page) and hang it prominently in the classroom.

I then run through my consequences. I further explain that I will not take more than one minute in the initial incursion. It will either be resolved or it will become an issue to be continued after school.

I draw my consequences primarily from my school's discipline plan. However, I always add the caveat that I can circumvent the process whenever I believe the situation warrants it. I can escalate or de-escalate the consequences. I usually start with a warning which is accompanied by clear, direct eye contact. This is totally contrary to the approach of many of the discipline gurus. They say that you shouldn't make eye contact because it feeds into and continues the confrontation. The gurus, who are usually psychologists and social scientists, might be correct in theory; but they probably didn't grow up as a long shot in an urban, ghetto, underperforming area. Where I come from, as a long shot, not making eye contact is a sign of weakness, and it unleashes more chaos, not less. In essence, if you get punked out in your classroom and try to just move on, don't expect to remain the leader.

If the warning is ineffective, I don't play musical chairs. I don't change seat assignments. I don't use the stars and check system. I don't believe in writing names on the board for negative behavior. In fact, I don't usually write names on the board at all. There are two principle reasons why I refrain from the use of this strategy. One, I don't intend to have so many disciplinary problem students that I can't remember to whom I issued what consequences; and two, I don't want to give long shots any negative press. For them, writing down their names is often synonymous with celebrity. Also, if consequences are issued to more than two or three students during a one-hour class, the time it takes for warnings, writing their names on the board, and placement of all the annoying stars, numbers, letters, and checks could cost you up to half of the sacred minutes of learning time. I am of the firm belief that it is the lost learning time stemming from a lack of relationship-building that causes low performance, not a lack of trained teachers.

For long shots, having their names on the board is even better than having to strategically place secretive tags (gang graffiti) throughout your classroom. They want the other students to think that they're outrageous, and with their names plastered on the board, you are assisting in the validation of the assertion. It might as well be a wanted poster. I go from the warning directly to detention in most cases, which includes the initiating of the teacher-student mediation process. (This process will be discussed in detail in the next section.)

I love and live for detention. The reason that I derive so much pleasure from it is this: Detention is my opportunity to spend some individual time getting into the student's head. It's one of the best opportunities for relationship-building that you'll ever have. It's your opportunity to open up, get real, expose your goal and agenda, and check their madness. It's a perfect time and place to debunk their underdeveloped logic and dispel their erroneous myths. It's also an excellent opportunity to hear where they are coming from, as well. Every urban public school ought to have a formal school detention program for tardiness, truancy, and other infractions. But beyond the formal detention, each and every individual teacher should conduct their own after-school detention. When structured properly, it will eliminate many of your in-class miseries.

If detention fails, I will call or send a letter to the student's home. I usually do this for documentation, not help, although some parent contacts have proven beneficial. The reason I say that I don't contact the parent for help is simple. In general, when contacting the home of a long shot, there are normally two types of parents that you will encounter. The first type is the enabler, who will support their kid's rich fantasy life and blame the teacher, and the second type is the genuinely concerned but overwhelmed and nearly defeated parent. Although the first type of parent occurs with some regularity, in the vast majority of cases, it's the second type of parent that I have encountered. So when you make contact, just know that, for the most part, real assistance is unlikely. Also, don't spend much time worrying about being the bearer of bad news. When you make contact, in most cases, it will not come as a surprise to the parent. Realistically, by the time the student is in ninth, tenth, or eleventh grade, the parent already knows the types of behaviors that are being displayed at school, because similar behaviors are generally being manifested at home. Most parents of urban underperforming students already know when their kids are knuckleheads; they just don't know what to do about it. In many instances, the parents will end up asking you for advice, direction, and assistance.

If all of the other interventions fail, I will suspend the student from my class in accordance with state education code and ask the principal to intervene. (In California, a teacher can suspend for one and one-half days—the day of the infraction and the next day.) This is where it is important to have true administrative support. If the counselor at your school is a supportive ally and a trained relationship-builder, you should consider a consultation. However, if they are not, you should try to eliminate them from the discipline process. From my experience in urban underperforming schools, most counselors tended to come up with the same old dubious, psychology-based strategies that have been ineffective over the past thirty years. In many cases, the kids even know that it's a deception, and they use the counselor as a tool to thwart the teacher's efforts. On numerous occasions, in order to avoid facing the potential of real consequences, students have asked to be sent to the counselor or walked out and gone there themselves. They obviously know where their manipulation is more likely to yield results.

Here are a few more reasons to be cautious about referring discipline issues to counselors. All of the research I have read indicates that school counseling is an American invention that was created during the Industrial Revolution. It was designed to address the potential problems produced by an influx of students from rural locations into urban centers. The counselors of old were not touted as trained student specialists like today, but were regular teachers who basically taught classes centered on moral, ethical, and academic guidance. Further, I could find no statistical evidence to verify that they have been an effective entity in urban education.

Moreover, in my experience, counselors in urban underperforming schools are usually *not* ex-long shots, and many are not even products of urban public schools. Therefore, instead of approaching the situation from a culturally intuitive perspective, they often attempt to employ strategies and procedures based on theoretical models or their own gut feelings, which are frequently incompatible with the experience of urban students. Also, sending the student to the counselor often leads to false perceptions. Because the counselor is typically housed in the administrative offices, the student often perceives them as the next step in the discipline process and above the teacher. This leads to a further erosion of the teacher's authority. What's more, with a few notable exceptions, every counselor I've ever met has described her job as being a student advocate, not a supporter of the educational process. Normally they listen to the student, then attempt to resolve the issue by placing the teacher and the student on the same level. Frequently, they try to cast the issue as a personality clash or a conflict between adversaries with antithetical viewpoints. And in the end, more often than not, the teacher is left feeling as though he or she has been interrogated, vilified, and classified as some sort of student saboteur.

Further, I am aware that counselors and therapists serve different functions; however, in this case, the implications are the same. In an article entitled "Therapists Enfeebling the Nation," syndicated columnist George Will makes several great points about the industry as a whole. Will, who is seen by many educators as a right-wing ultra-conservative, asserts that from childhood the "grief industry" has promoted what they hold up as emotionally healthy behaviors. These behaviors include actions like inventorying your feelings and venting. The industry, according to the article, continues to do this even though "abundant research indicates no connection between high self-esteem and high [academic] achievement." Mr. Will goes on to introduce the concept of "unearned self-esteem" as being a more critical problem. In the end, he practically charges the industry with duplicity because of their "professional stake in [supporting] the myth that most people are too fragile to cope with life's vicissitudes and traumas without professional help." This type of potential enabling is wrong for urban underperforming schools.

In general, I think that the counselors in urban settings really don't know what to do; and that's not a slam. In reality, most of the staff members are in the same predicament. Remember, most urban underperforming staff members are not ex-long shots. However, instead of admitting it, counselors appear to strive to insure that the buck doesn't stop with them. Subsequently, they often redirect the students back to the teacher, with nothing done. Then they quickly jump on the blame-the-teacher bandwagon as a cover-up. Perhaps it's different at high-performing schools, but in urban settings, that's what I've observed. So, unless the counselors at your school have been retrained in a teacher-supportive, relationship-building tradition, you should rely on a solid educational philosophy, a comprehensive discipline plan, and then your licensed administrators.

While on the topic of who not to rely on for help, I believe that campus security is far more detrimental than useful. Similar to the counselor, they undermine the teacher's respect and authority, and they do very little to make the campus environment safe. In my experience, the vast majority of security staffers tend to openly criticize teachers for what they perceive as not maintaining discipline in the classroom. But what they fail to understand is this: in many cases, it is because of their presence that the students act out in the first place. The long shots know that it is illegal for teachers to physically remove them (and they shouldn't have to) from class. They know that the procedure is that security, the counselor, the vice-principal, the dean, or somebody must be called. So, the time between the call for security and their arrival becomes prime time for ratcheting up the behavior even more. When security does arrive, the elevated drama and threats of force, handcuffs, and other restraining devices set the stage for an even greater drama. This completes the long shot's goal of securing his status as a gangster. In place of security, we must implement more relationship-building activities. We must implement clear-cut rules and standards for behavior, and we must impose and vigorously enforce consequences for violators. In essence, each staff member must become the preserver of a safe and secure environment. The faint of heart need not apply. If a real crime has been committed, real police should handle it. Security in the urban underperforming schools more often than not usurps the teachers' authority and feeds the long shot's ego.

If you have credibility with your principal, vice-principal, or dean, I encourage you to constantly nurture the relationship. Go to them when there is a truly unresolved issue. And when you go, don't go begging. Already have a strategy in mind that can be backed up by a theory and logical methodology.

As dean, I always try to ask the teachers if they have some specific instructions or outcome they're seeking or if they want me to come to a decision in the matter. Whenever possible, I try to recommend teacher-student mediation as part of the solution. In this process, the teacher is allowed to maintain credibility as the leader, get to know the student, and come up with a workable solution. I also try not to involve another staff member as mediator. I will mediate student-to-student issues, but never teacher-to-student. That way the student doesn't perceive another authority is going to step in on his behalf and undermine the teacher. Staff unity must be consistent and clear. I believe in teacher-to-student mediation. I believe in it so strongly I created a special mediation program that was implemented at Gompers High School with pretty amazing results. The process and results will be discussed in the next section.

Teacher-Student Mediation Process Model (TSMP)

At Gompers High School, I was fortunate enough to have an opportunity to work with a principal, Donald Mitchell, who was courageous enough to acknowledge that the status quo was unacceptable. Mr. Mitchell, who had hired me as a teacher several years earlier at the district's zero-tolerance school, told me that he was open to trying new and innovative approaches to decrease conflict and violence and improve student success. When I attempted to discuss my duties and responsibilities with him, instead of handing me an elaborately unattainable job description, he sent me away to assist in the creation of a program to accomplish the goal. When I returned, after listening to my thoughts on the potential effectiveness of a program based on restorative justice through mediation, he gave the okay to implement it.

Fortunately for me, I didn't have to create a program from scratch. I already knew of a mediation model that I felt could be modified to suit our needs. After I ended my career in law enforcement, I worked for the Victim Offender Reconciliation Program (VORP) of the Central Valley in Fresno, California. There, I became a certified mediator and worked as the program's case manager. The VORP process takes a three-pronged approach to conflict resolution—recognition, restoration, and relationship building. In the process, the victim and offender are brought face to face to discuss the injustice, restore equity (make things right, whether through monetary restitution, apologies, or other considerations), and establish future intentions (relationship guidelines). The entire process is facilitated by a trained mediator. (In order to receive a mediation certificate, a training program must be completed and three cases successfully mediated.)

With all of this training behind me, it only made sense that I design the Gompers model after VORP. Initially, I designed the program for mediations between students, with me functioning as the mediator. In the first year of the program, I completed approximately fifty mediations that involved a total of ninety-seven individuals. At the end of the school year, it was clear that the program had had a serious impact at my school site, substantially reducing campus tensions with no apparent downside. In fact, of the ninety-seven persons who participated in the mediation process, none of the individuals ended up in a physical confrontation, and only two persons returned for follow-up assistance, which mostly consisted of clarifying their relational positions. In year two of the program, the number of mediations and campus fights dropped even further. The number of fights dropped to a number unheard of: five. That's right, five! And suspensions dropped by about seventy-five percent. For a school that was known throughout the district for riots, rebellions, and brawls, this was some feat.

Observing the benefits of the program, Mr. Mitchell approached me and asked if I would attempt to come up with a program that could be used directly in the classroom between teachers and students. This posed something of a challenge because in reality, what he was asking me to do was to train all the teachers to be mediators of their own disagreements, then to lead their own potential offenders through a process in hopes of resolving the conflict.

Interestingly enough, I didn't encounter many problems at all with the kids accepting the process, but the teachers were a different story. The teachers simply wanted to teach without being burdened and encumbered by unnecessary disruptions and pointless distractions. Justifiably, the teachers didn't want to be burdened with another administrative mandate. After taking all of this into consideration, I knew that if the teachers were to use the program, it had to be relatively easy to incorporate and, above all, effective. Every step of the way, right down to the name of the program, I was very careful not to offend or alienate the teachers. My putting the teacher first in my thinking gave them the assurance that the program was not just another train-and-blame tactic, but was about casting each of them in the role of campus leader while empowering and inviting the student to be part of the conflict resolution process. After some consideration, the Teacher-Student Mediation Program (TSMP) was born.

The program consists of two components—the student worksheet and the teacher-staff response and resolution sheet. On the front side of the student worksheet, it asks the student to explain in writing what happened in the conflict. The next section asks the student to write down what he or she feels could be done to make things right again. The final section asks the student to write down how he or she would respond in the future to this and similar situations if things were made right again. On the reverse side of the form, the student is provided with sections to list any questions or make any comments that they might have for the teacher. (See Appendix Forms B and C.)

After reading the student worksheet, the teacher is required to respond in writing and then conference with the student. The teacher-staff response and resolution sheet basically addresses the same points as the student worksheet. It then goes a step further. The teacher-staff response goes on to allow the teacher to explain what would make things right from his or her perspective and to give clear instructions on future expectations for that student in class. Finally, the teacher asks if more clarification is needed. If more discussion is required, the process continues on the reverse side of the document. If no further discussion is needed, the student and the teacher sign the document and celebrate the resolution. (See Appendix Forms D and E.)

In the early stages of implementation, the new program was put to the test. I could not have designed a better evaluation apparatus for the program. It simultaneously solidified the principal's and the teachers' belief in the process.

A black female student called a white male teacher every derogatory term that she could dream up. She then stormed out of class. On her way to my office, the student called home and left an inflammatory message for her mother.

In my office, I immediately provided the student with a TSMP student worksheet. After she completed the worksheet, I gave it to the teacher to complete the process. Before the teacher had a chance to completely finish the process, the mother arrived on campus, breathing fire and demanding to speak with the principal. The commotion was so loud that I could hear it in my office, which, at the time, was down the hall. After unsuccessful attempts to calm the parent, Mr. Mitchell brought her to my office to find out what I knew about the situation. I didn't have much to add, so the parent demanded to see the teacher, who was teaching a class at the time. I told the principal that the student had completed her portion of the mediation form and that it had been given to the teacher. I suggested that we retrieve the form.

After the mother read the form, she actually became embarrassed. She apologized to us and said it appeared as though her daughter had a serious problem that she would handle at home, and she no longer felt the need to talk with the teacher. When the teacher finished his part of the form, he and the student came to an agreement, and I heard nothing more from either of them for the remainder of the year. The process turned out to be a great way for a teacher to defuse and postpone conflicts in class, lay the framework for resolving issues at a more opportune time, create instant documentation of noteworthy incidents, and serve as a conduit for relationship building. In the final analysis, the teachers accepted the program, and again the results were impressive. I knew that the process was working when the teachers started coming to me and asking for the mediation sheets instead of the standard referrals. Also, I was somewhat encouraged when one teacher came to me and said that after mediation with one of his students, he realized he was at fault in the matter.

Conflict (the Chinese Model)

According to the Chinese, conflict is "A state of disharmony between incompatible or antithetical persons, ideas, or interests; a clash." In China, the term conflict consists of two characters—*chorng twu*—which represent danger and opportunity. The illustration that follows depicts the characters for "conflict."

At school, I often used this model when talking with students about their approach to managing their conflicts. Of course, I explained to them how, in most cases, they never got to a true resolution because they always focused on the possible danger involved and neglected the potential opportunity. But the more I used the model with the students, the more I thought about the teachers and staff.

The more I thought about this model, I realized that in many urban underperforming schools, the overwhelming majority of the personnel don't relationship-build, attempt to discipline, or resolve conflict for the same reason that the students failed to do it—the thought of the potential danger.

Urban underperforming school teachers and staff members must begin to think of conflict in the same manner as the Chinese. They must begin to bring a balanced approach to the table when dealing with the students. Sure, the potential for danger is always present, but the prospect for true relationship development is present as well.

If I can offer teachers one final piece of advice on discipline, it would be this: when confronted with the fight-or-flight impulse, somehow learn to discipline yourself. Show some restraint. Don't always choose the flight impulse. Urban underperforming kids know this avoidance behavior really well. They have been employing the strategy in one form or another throughout their entire lives. So when you don't take the moral high ground and do what they, and you, know is right to eliminate the foolishness, you lose your credibility. I'm not asking you to stare down a gun or knife, but I am asking you to step up when a long shot deliberately calls you out.

The key is ancient history. Be a little Chinese in your thought process. Give danger and opportunity equal billing in your decision-making practice.

Instruction:

a) Standards

b) Course Outline and Syllabus

c) Methods (SQ3Rq, and others)

d) Skill Building (note taking, etc.)

e) Projects (group, individual, homework, etc.)

f) Grading

There isn't much that I have to say about instruction. This is the area where the straight shots excel. They are great at creating instructional strategies, staff development programs, and workshop models. In fact, I have used many of the instructional strategies developed by the administrative straights. After a solid relationship has been established and the landscape has been cleared of the long-shot distractions, many of the strategies actually do work. So, with that said, here is my brief take on instruction.

Good instruction is very important. It fills the void left behind after clearing up the long-shot distractions. Without good instruction to fill the void created by the implementation of a high-quality, discipline-based, relationship-building program, things will fall apart fast. Discipline in and of itself is not a panacea. In the Bible, it says, "When an evil spirit comes out of a man, it goes through arid places seeking rest and does not find it. Then it says, 'I will return to the house I left.' When it arrives, it finds the house swept clean and put in order. Then, it goes and takes seven other spirits more wicked than itself, and they go in and live there. And the final condition of that man is worse than the first" (Luke 11:24-26, NIV). Failing to fill the void created by relationship-building is a recipe for disaster. Good instruction fills the empty space.

Standards

Standards are here to stay, and that's fine by me. Whether district, state, or national, we have arrived at a time in society where a computable model with benchmarks, criteria, and touchstones will be the yardstick for measuring student achievement. I won't attempt to argue for or against standards because, frankly, I think they are useful. I suggest a meeting with your department chair and any other instructional leaders at your disposal. They can direct you to and, in some cases, instruct you on, the latest diagnostic tools. With this said, I would encourage all teachers to construct their lesson plans with their district standards in mind. I would also encourage a course outline and class syllabus.

Course Outline and Syllabus

A course syllabus and general outline are indispensable parts of the instructional planning process. The course syllabus provides an overview and framework for fulfillment and completion of the outline. A typical syllabus should contain the course objective, course components, scoring rubrics or guides, a grading scale, an acknowledgement section (for students and parents to sign), and an instructor contact section.

The outline, on the other hand, is a general course road map. It should be used in much the same way as a compass, to lay out the direction and theme of the course. The outline should, at a minimum, contain the name of the course, the chapters of work that will be covered, the testing cycle, a specific time structure, and any other pertinent time-sensitive data. For example, during the first two weeks of World History 1, chapters ten and eleven, the first twenty vocabulary words, and the first test will be completed. This cycle is then repeated to cover the entire semester.

Beyond these two directional guides, for the seriously structured and slightly masochistic, I also recommend a very short daily lesson plan. I hear some school districts now demand them, but in most districts I think the verdict is still out on whether it is a legitimate request. However, if you do decide to have a plan, it should break the day's lesson down into the number of activities and the time allotted for each specific activity. The daily plan serves several purposes—it serves as a strategic guide for the teacher in the fulfillment of the standards; it's also a great time-management strategy. Further, it provides the students with structure, and in case of your absence, it serves as a built-in substitute teacher plan. The plan should include sections covering the standards and objectives for the day and the materials needed to fulfill them. It should also list the chronological procedure that should be followed and an assessment or evaluation section. If the students are oriented properly and the necessary jobs distributed, your goal for each day should be met.

Methods and Skill Building

Beyond the course outline, class syllabus, and the daily lesson plan, teachers should establish and introduce some type of methods and skills for general study. These techniques should help students to synthesize material in a speedy and orderly manner. There are hundreds of methods out there. For example, when I teach, I often use a modified version of the SQ3R study strategy. The acronym stands for survey, question, read, recite, and review. (For more information on study methods, go to any of the major search engine web sites and enter SQ3R and other study methods, and you'll get about a million hits.) I like the SQ3R method but feel as though it left out a key element in the process, so I modified it. In the classroom, I called it SQ3Rq, with the small q standing for quiz. After using the strategy, I immediately followed up with a two- or three-question quiz, nothing too stressful. Find some methods and make them work for you.

As far as note-taking skills and strategies go, if the students have already embraced a method, I have usually allowed them to employ whatever technique they learned. Many of the students seemed to already be familiar with Cornell Notes. But if they had no set strategy, I would teach them to use one that I came up with, the reduction and color coding technique. In this strategy, for roughly every ten to twelve pages of text materials, I expected to see the students reduce it to about one page of notes. I also asked students to use colored markers to indicate sections, page numbers, names, dates, and events. This strategy also turned out to be a great organizational tool. Just as with study methods, note-taking strategies can easily be found on-line.

In most cases, underperforming urban public school students don't do much homework. So, instead of fighting the funk, be creative. I used, and highly recommend, homework projects. In my district, a semester consisted of about eighteen weeks. As a history teacher, I would assign three projects, with one coming due every six weeks. (I don't think there should be much of a problem adapting projects to other courses.) Each student would be required to complete three different projects—a collage, a historical display, and the reading of a course-related textbook. An essay had to accompany the collage and the display, while an essay and completed reading logs accompanied the textbook project. The order of completion would be left to the student's discretion. So, if a student was more comfortable making a collage, the collage could be completed first. The successful completion of one project usually provided the confidence to try the next. As far as project assistance, I supplied only three things—an abundance of classroom displays from former students, the scoring rubrics, and periodic check-ins for suggestions. Projects work well in individual and group settings. When giving projects as homework assignments, the completion rate was ninety-five percent or higher. (On the following page, a sample homework project rubric has been inserted.)

HOMEWORK PROJECT RUBRICS

Collage Project Rubric

Requirements	Checklist	Points Possible	Points Scored
Cover the entire collage surface. There should be no background paper showing.	_____	25	_____
Write a one-page paper showing proof that your idea came from the text (chapter, page, etc.).	_____	25	_____
The paper must also explain your reason(s) for selecting the theme.	_____	25	_____
The paper must be typed, and it must have a beginning, middle, and end.	_____	25	_____
Totals	**Checks Completed: Y / N**	**100**	**Score:** _____

Historical Display Rubric

Requirements	Checklist	Points Possible	Points Scored
The display must demonstrate thoughtful construction.	_____	50	_____
Write a half-page summary explaining your project; also show proof that your idea came from the text (chapter, page, etc.).	_____	25	_____
The paper must be typed.	_____	25	_____
Totals	**Checks Completed: Y / N**	**100**	**Score:** _____

Course-Related Text Rubric

Requirements	Checklist	Points Possible	Points Scored
Read and keep course-related textbook logs.	_____	40	_____
Write a five-paragraph, two-page essay critiquing the book.	_____	40	_____
The essay must be typed, and it must have a clear beginning, middle, and end.	_____	10	_____
The essay must contain no more than three composition errors.	_____	10	_____
Totals	**Checks Completed: Y / N**	**100**	**Score:** _____

Note: *For all projects, see the class examples, and consult with fellow students, before seeking advice from the teacher.*

Grading

Grading is more than a district benchmark. For urban underperforming students, it can be a validation of who they are as people. Oftentimes, urban students will attempt to play the indifference game, but don't let that fool you; they care about their grades. However, when they feel helpless to change them or afraid of appearing stupid, or even worse, weak, they'll pretend that grades are insignificant and irrelevant.

I am totally opposed to the notion of giving grades to falsely protect students' so-called "self-esteem." In fact, I'm one hundred percent against any and all forms of grade inflation and social promotion. In the long run, it doesn't benefit the recipient at all. However, I am also against making grading an all-or-nothing event.

To me, it makes more practical sense to numerically score students for what they can do, separately from the overall performance. So when I score, I set a course benchmark (for example, 70 raw points during the semester = "C") and focus on the accumulation of the points. For example, a single test may count for a maximum of six (6) points. Therefore, if there were fifty questions on the test and a student answered twenty-two correctly, the score for that student is 2.64 points (towards the goal of 70), not an F. Here is how I arrived at the score: $(22 / 50) 6 = 2.64$.

If a student is going to fail (and I have had my share of failures), he or she will still fail using a system like this one. However, with this system, the students at least get the opportunity to imagine the possibilities and to think of themselves as potentially being in the game. Using this system, I have also had many documented successes. One of my most memorable was with a student during my first year of teaching at the Elkhorn Juvenile Correctional Facility (Boot Camp), in Fresno, CA. This Laotian student, convicted of auto theft, initially performed at such a low skill level in everything that I questioned whether he could cut it or not. I diagnosed his problem as being something similar to my own as a child: academic disconnect. Although our problems derived from different sources, mine from making a conscious choice to miss school and his due to the fact that he moved so much (six or seven different schools in five or six years), the end result was the same. After receiving a 1.9 or so on his first history test, a test that had a maximum score of five (5) points, this guy was beaming. Speaking in his flawed English, he told me, "I almost got a two; now, I only need only sixty-eight point now; I can do better next time!" I wasn't about to dampen his spirits by telling him that he had scored thirty-eight percent. In the end, I can say without reservation that that student left the ranks of the long shots. He passed the class and became something of an academic leader at the camp. When I moved to San Diego, he and several other Boot Camp cadets wrote letters to keep me abreast of their progress and to thank me for teaching them. Grading should be structured to build optimism first and then to assess skill level.

Curriculum Moves

In underperforming schools, students tend to latch on to any superficial fad, trendy concept, or chic advertising scheme that comes along. They try desperately to play the role of the "Big Baller." They live to make a fashion statement; they die to be in style. A few students have, to the best of their ability, given the situation some rational thought and have perceived that "the business of America is business." But what they don't seem to grasp is how to legitimately take hold of the philosophy.

For the most part, students in urban underperforming schools don't understand the intricacies and nuances of the business world. In general, they don't know that businesses are promoting their own best interests and that corporations pay the media to manipulate them. They don't know that lobbyists court the government to support their enterprises, and the vast majority of them don't even grasp that the media is a business. On television, I recently heard a conversation between a news interviewer and a fashion designer. According to the designer, the style for girls' jeans was about to change. The low-fitting, bikini-cut look is to be replaced by the new style that will be approximately two to three inches higher. The designer even tossed in a bit of reverse psychology as she attempted to persuade her young audience to embrace the change. Instead of haranguing the fashion industry for creating and profitably marketing the jeans in the first place, the designer blamed the jeans, as though they had lowered themselves. She said that the two- to three-inch change was a good decision because jeans of today had become practically indecent. Just think about it. With media assistance and the tacit approval of our laissez-faire government, this single designer was in the midst of promoting the next business cycle for the fashion industry.

The reason that this travesty is being played out is simple: urban underperforming schools major in the minors. Underperforming schools attempt to teach students reading, writing, math, science, and history, but fail to deliver a compelling reason for participating in the enterprise. Majoring in the majors would consist of intertwining the subject matter into a clear-cut, logical process that leads directly to financial security in America. In brief, students are not taught about the workings of government, how to be business-minded and media-savvy. Instead, they are taught by the media and their peer group to be consumers. After awhile, it all becomes a vicious, self-regenerating cycle: the producer names the tune, the media uses celebrities to promote it, consumers buy into the conspicuous consumption, and, when maximum profits have been realized, the producer changes the tune and begins the process anew.

When one considers all of the sophisticated campaigns, strategies, and tactics that are being used against urban youth, and the fact that most urban underperforming schools do absolutely nothing to counter them, it's a miracle that the students leave school with anything that resembles an education.

Certainly there are those who disagree with me. Many of them will say that urban underperforming students have access to the same education as high performers and simply don't take advantage of it. In a sense, they are right. In many cases, urban underperforming students do have access to the same education. The issue, however, is not the access and comparability but the embracing and utilization of the instruction.

Most students in high-performing schools embrace and use the instruction. That's why we call them high performers in the first place. The obvious question is: Why does one group buy into the education model while the other does not? I think there is a simple explanation.

In general, students who have grown up exposed to the American business model are far more inclined to embrace academic instruction of any kind. The American business model is a natural part of life for high performing communities. Therefore, the students live and breathe the achievement-by-means-of-education model daily. They can also attest to its success. In most high-performing schools, the students see what their parents have accomplished through education and use it as a catalyst for their labors. Consequently, for many of them, attending a class with rigorous instruction is the general expectation. However, because of the unfamiliar nature of the model, urban underperforming students are more likely to view the same subject matter as boring, too hard, or just the next dose of mind-numbing rhetoric—especially when districts, like the one where I'm employed, wait until their senior year to introduce them to courses like government and economics. By then, the students have already become media zombies and are preparing to receive master's degrees in the consumer tango.

In order to break this cycle, urban underperforming schools should add at least two classes to the course curriculum: "Philosophy and Religion" and "Government, Business and the Media." These courses should be taught several times throughout a student's academic career. The courses would assist students in complex, critical thinking and decision-making skills. They would also insure that the students have an understanding of the American business model. And lastly, the courses will help reveal the significance of education as a relevant component for their future success.

The philosophy portion of the course should cover as many of the major theories and thinkers as possible—Chinese, Greek, Indian, and Western. The religion segment should focus on various world religions, including atheism, agnosticism, Buddhism, Christianity, Confucianism, Deism, Hinduism, Islam, Judaism, Shinto, Zoroastrianism, and more. The government and business portion of the second course should deal with subject matter pertaining to the functioning of the federal, state, and local government, principles of accounting, investing, banking, and home ownership. The media segment should focus on teaching students to become discretionary connoisseurs of propaganda. The course should also provide an understanding of the influence, power, and persuasion of marketing and advertising on their lives.

The Teacher *(You and Your Persona)*

- Who are You, and how do you perceive yourself in the environment?
- What is your style, and is it right for your audience?
- Material Knowledge and Instructional Skills are not enough.
- Job # 1 (Inspiration)
- Conflict anyone?
- Get the Top-Dawg Syndrome

Who are you, and how do you perceive yourself in the environment?

"Know thyself" was the admonishment of the oracle of Apollo at Delphi. We have all heard these insightful words of Greek wisdom; however, when applied to persons interested in becoming urban underperforming school teachers, hearing is not enough. Adhering to this admonishment is nearly essential. All who desire to teach in an urban public school must, without a doubt, know who they are; furthermore, they must also have an accurate perception of themselves within the environment, or woe unto them.

Urban underperforming environments are in a constant state of simmering chaotic fluctuation. There is no room for uncertainty in the setting. In high-performing schools, students come to school with a generous degree of acculturation and discipline. This acculturation is a byproduct of a stable history of academic and financial security, parental leadership, and moral guidance. As a result, chaos is kept to a minimum. In urban underperforming schools, this process is virtually nonexistent; therefore, the teacher must be the stabilizing force. In order to be this force, the teacher must have an understanding of the phenomenon, or be willing and able to learn on the job. That is why it is important to "know thyself."

This constant state of fluctuation, which includes a high level of transient movement, the potential for violence, and an anti-education edge, generally leads to pathetic attempts on the part of the school staff members to save, stabilize, or protect themselves. The attempted stabilization often causes the staff to break into cliques, factions, and camps. Once they are divided, that's when the power grabbing commences. Individuals, and each and every group or faction, vie for their piece of the power. When this occurs, the entire school is reduced to internal-political power brokering which ultimately assists in destroying the learning community.

In the final analysis, the power brokering reveals the emergence of the urban underperforming school pecking order. The order usually consists of a combination of lower-level administrators, followed by clericals/classroom aides, then security/campus supervision, custodial staff, and, lastly, teachers. Who actually controls the power at the school may periodically change; however, there is one somewhat constant fact: it is never the teachers. And the students know it. Some of them are even brazen enough to tell you to your face.

I think teachers end up at the bottom of the pecking order for several reasons. The first is the nature of teachers and their general belief in sacrifice (i.e. low salaries, donated time, and out-of-pocket school-related purchases). The second reason is the general attitude held towards teachers by administrators. Teachers appear to be so disrespected that the students sense it and simply follow their lead. And finally, it could have to do with the teachers' own voluntary abdication of authority, which is usually based on their general belief that things change. That is, when it comes to challenging the establishment, many teachers have a "this too shall pass" mentality (i.e. the next new and improved strategy will come along, or a district régime change will occur) instead of a confrontationally demanding of respect attitude.

Additionally, in urban underperforming schools, there is a great deal of manipulation going on. There are district games, like the forced implementation of hastily-contrived programs based on, and modeled after, the latest research; there are individual site games, like train and blame; there are teacher games, like pass'em and push'em forward; there are parent games like special ed. and immigration fraud; and there are student games, like Billy Bad-Ass, Marley the Marijuana Man, Tran the Asian-Mexican-Black Tagging Man, Biggy-Snoop-TuPac the Fifty-Cent rapper-lover, and so on. There's so much going on that even the teachers who are up to speed about the antics get tired after awhile. One can only imagine what it must be like for a teacher who comes to work in an environment such as this without being rooted, grounded, or trained in its ways. A good many of them simply freak out. And when that happens, they are ripe for a flip. By this I mean that the individual is a prime target for being victimized. In other words, the person may become a pawn to be maneuvered about instead of an academically-steady force to be reckoned with. And if or when this occurs, that teacher or staff member becomes totally useless to the school.

An urban underperforming school is no place to go seeking an identity. In this setting, we need people who are uniquely prepared for the encounter, and your beliefs must be suitable for the type of relationship-building needed in the environment. Urban public schools don't need someone who is better suited for one of the high-performing locations. So, don't think that because you were successful in a high-performing environment, the same degree of success will be experienced at an urban underperformer. A totally different set of skills is required for each.

My advice to any teacher who is thinking about working in an urban, public, underperforming school is this: make sure that you know who you are going in. I would also recommend an accurate assessment of your tolerance level for long shots and all of their antics. I would further recommend that you be clear about your degree of tolerance for observing academic carnage. With travesties like inadequate instruction time, inflated grades, and social promotions running rampant, an accurate assessment is vital. And lastly, I would really recommend a back-up plan, just in case you can't hang in there. I've seen many teachers quit mid-semester and just walk away, and that's all right. However, I've also seen those who were clearly in over their heads try to stay and tolerate it because they had no back-up plan. Some ended up on stress leave, or even worse, as some long shot's trick.

When thinking about the notion of becoming a long shot's trick, one potentially serious incident comes readily to mind. While working at ALBA, the zero-tolerance school, a very young female teacher appeared to have her foundation gradually unravel as the year advanced. Her behavior, as time passed, more and more began to resemble a person suffering from Stockholm Syndrome. (Stockholm Syndrome is a condition where a hostage starts to identify and sympathize with their captor.) It got so bad that the teacher was willing to violate the law. After being expressly told that it was illegal to take students who were suspended or expelled onto a comprehensive high school campus, she continued to use her vehicle to take several teenaged boys to high school baseball games. Shortly thereafter, things got worse. Somehow, provocative pictures of her students' genitalia began to surface, and it was concluded that they were taken with her camera. Fortunately for her, the media never got hold of the story, and the end of the school year was drawing near. The next year, she didn't return. So be sure of yourself when you decide to become a teacher at an urban underperformer.

Beyond figuring out who you are, the next thing you should focus on is how you perceive yourself in the environment. How you perceive yourself in the environment is just as important as knowing who you are. Many new teachers, both young and old, often see themselves as rescuers, redeemers, or saviors of "those" kids. They don't usually last too long. I, for one, am glad about it. The redeemer-savior conjures up too many negative thoughts of mission-style colonialism and Bureau of Indian Affairs-style assimilation efforts. These teachers are as unneeded at urban underperformers as the racist teacher, who, by the way, sometimes ends up there. Urban underperformers don't need any more of the victimization and prejudice that comes with people who still perceive it as the white man's burden to rescue the blacks, browns, and yellows of the world. What urban underperformers need is stable, relationship-building, academically sound, committed individuals.

What is your style, and is it right for your audience?

Some might think that race plays a significant role in the turning around of urban underperforming schools, and consequently they advocate more same-race instructors. After careful consideration, however, I don't think this opinion is valid. As a black male who has taught in California classrooms for more than eight years where I was always in the minority, with Mexicans, Southeast Asians (Hmong, Vietnamese, Thai, and Cambodians), North Africans (Somali and Eritrean), Samoans, and Filipinos dominating the landscape, it was abundantly clear to me that my blackness alone was not enough to effect a change. Over time, I had even stood by and observed blacks and other ethnic minority race teachers be reduced to rubble by students from their own race. So race clearly wasn't much of a factor. In the final analysis, I concluded that style and audience connection were much more important—relationship, not race.

When I work with urban underperforming middle and high school students, initially my style is ghetto autocratic to the max. I will confront every slight. I make the leash as short as I can without stifling the group's creativity, and I continuously assert and promote myself as leader. But as time passes and as the nature of the environment reveals itself, I become increasingly more down-to-earth pragmatic. However, regardless of the circumstance, I never become an unrestrained liberal egalitarian. In fact, I go out of my way to make sure that the long shots know that at the core of it all, I'm still the leader, and I can unilaterally rescind their civil liberties. No anger, no hostility—just the reality. I then set out to assure the slings and straight shots that my contention as benevolent sole proprietor and ultimate landlord is not a deception, but the real deal.

Having the right style for the audience is paramount. In urban underperforming schools, if there is an audience mismatch, the black version of the thug life will be no more effective than the white version of patriotic pomp and circumstance. The style must fit the audience. This is a simple lesson that I learned growing up with a dad who was an itinerant Southern Baptist preacher. Although the audiences were always completely composed of black folk, if he failed to employ a style that engaged their particular circumstance, you knew it instantly. There would be a deafening quiet throughout the church. And the mismatch would be confirmed by the hollow echo coming from the collection bucket. No emotional screaming and shouting and no jubilant bellows of "Amen" meant no Washingtons and Lincolns, and for sure, no Jacksons, Hamiltons or Franklins.

With this in mind, here is my style. As stated, after assessing the group, initially I maintain my domain as an autocracy. I have found that by taking this stance as an initial position, I get enough respect from the long shots to at least afford me the opportunity to present my introductory programming. After this, if I've received a reasonable buy-in from a sufficient number of longs, I then become more culturally pragmatic. In short, I become somewhat of an urban chameleon—flexible enough to adapt and change based on the audience while maintaining a predatory protective edge. Your choice of style will ultimately determine your ability to build relationships. Choose it carefully.

Material knowledge and instructional strategies are not enough.

Let me begin this section by reassuring the instructional strategy preparation organizations—university teacher education programs, teacher credentialing and certification programs, school district curriculum and professional developers, and the like—that their domains are safe. We absolutely need their program services. When I say that material instruction is not enough, I mean that training in the instruction methodology and dissemination practices is vital, but it's only a part of the whole; it is not the sum of the essentials.

The extraordinary pursuit of a teaching credential, at least in California, is uncanny, and especially when taking into consideration that it's practically useless in determining who is likely to be an effective teacher in urban underperforming schools. At best, the current approach measures only one side of the equation—academic proficiency. Student teaching is supposed to cover the rest; but how many teachers do their student teaching in urban underperforming schools? Very few! And the ones that do immediately recognize the relationship mismatch, and upon completion, do everything in their power not to return as permanent teachers.

I couldn't believe all of the obstacles I was confronted with in order to get a teaching credential in California. When I moved to the west coast, I already had a master's degree, but it wasn't in the social sciences—history, government, economics, and psychology. So the state required that I take a subject matter competence test, the Single Subject Assessments for Teaching—SSAT.

Under the circumstances, I felt that California's demand for the SSAT was only prudent. But, as I quickly learned, the SSAT wasn't the first step. Prior to taking the SSAT, I had to take the California Basic Education Skills Test—CBEST.

After passing both tests, I thought I was on my way. Then my teacher education program advisor at Fresno Pacific University informed me that I would also be required to take, and pass, another assessment test called The Praxis Series. This test was designed to measure data similar to the SSAT, but in a different format. Unlike the true-false and multiple choice SSAT format, the Praxis questions required that the answers be submitted in essay form. I ended up paying for and taking that damned test three times. By the way, I passed the test every single time; but there was something called a "low pass," which meant you passed but you didn't. I know several ex-long shots that have been taking the test for years and haven't passed. (Recently in California, the SSAT and the Praxis were combined into a single test called the CSET—the California Subject Examination for Teachers.)

After completing the Praxis, I had to complete the Fresno Pacific University's teacher education program's coursework, which consisted of six courses (twenty-seven units), plus a year of student teaching in order to get the five-year Preliminary Single Subject Teaching Credential. During the next five years, while working under the preliminary credential, the next requirement is to complete the necessary coursework in order to receive the Professional Clear Credential. This consisted of nine more classes (twenty-eight units). I completed this work at the University of California, San Diego (UCSD). And I still wasn't done.

In order to renew the professional clear, I had to complete 150 hours of professional growth. In the professional growth classes and workshops, the focus, again, was always on strategies for delivering instruction. The latest strategy being emphasized is the small school movement. According to this strategy, things will get better if the larger campuses are divided into smaller units (while still being housed on the same campus). The smaller units receive a designated focus or objective like engineering or computer technology. Other strategies of the past have included the Blue Print for Student Success—a reading and math dominated plan; SDAIE, or Specially Designed Academic Instruction in English; CLAD, a cultural language development skills strategy; the Socratic Method, a strategy of exploring a series of questions related to the investigation of the subject at hand; and Scaffolding, a strategy where knowledge is built layer upon layer until task mastery is achieved. There were also a host of reading strategies, including the Read Aloud, Silent Reading, and Guided Reading; and my all-time favorite, mini-lessons, a strategy of presenting the lessons in short, ten-to-fifteen-minute sound bites.

I got so fed up with the madness in a professional development workshop once that I snapped. The presenter was a likable enough person. But although she was highly credentialed, her demeanor and strategic beliefs left me with questions about her ability to survive in an urban underperforming environment. As she embarked on what seemed like a thirty-minute tirade about the rationale and purpose of the mini-lesson, I could practically feel my blood pressure rising. She said that the research indicated that, as a result of the television age, our students had very short attention spans. Therefore, lessons should be planned like a television program, with commercial breaks or a change in activities every ten to fifteen minutes. She went on to say that the lessons needed to be not only short, but engaging. What the presenter was saying almost made perfect sense, and the straight shot teachers were eating it up. But I wasn't buying it. Because what the presenter was really saying was that as a result of television viewing, our students were so undisciplined that they couldn't focus for more than a few minutes at a time. And what the engagement piece really meant was that she was asking us to become entertainers.

This entertainment approach over time would do no more than stifle the creativity of the students, and, in the future, demand more and more entertaining stunts by teachers; and in the end, the students would still most likely claim boredom. I grew up watching *Leave It to Beaver,* and I think that my generation was fairly creative. The show was in black and white, and the plot was simple but filled with innuendo and moral lessons. If anything extra like Technicolor or garish language was to be included, we had to create it ourselves via the imagination. The youth of today are so saturated with special effects, elaborate animations, degenerate language, and pyrotechnical displays that they have become unimaginative and uncreative. This state of over-saturation most certainly causes urban underperforming students to view academic rigor as boring. But that's no reason to alter the educational process; it's more of a reason to reintroduce the notion of discipline and creativity.

I challenged the presenter on the viability of her approach. My thinking was more along this line: there were high-performing schools out there where the students watched just as much television as our students, yet they didn't require mini-lessons. Also, in college, professors' lectures didn't include commercial breaks and pauses for station identification every fifteen minutes, and yet most students hung in there. So the issue almost certainly had nothing to do with the television age. It probably had more to do with the reverence that came with a positive, respectful relationship. Therefore, if we spent more time on relationship-building and less on acquiescing to theoretical constructs and entertainment schemes, we could conceivably present thoughtful, academically enriching **maxi-**lessons.

Realizing that I was at my limit, the principal stopped the workshop and took me out for a walk. To her credit, she promised that she would bring somebody in the next time who would address the social-relational dynamics in underperforming environments, and she did. The principal brought in a behavioral psychologist who came pretty close in his assessment of the dilemma, but he offered no concrete strategies or remedies for immediate implementation. I don't think it would have mattered much if he had, because the teachers didn't seem that interested. The interest level was so low that the principal had to step in a few times and remind the staff that we were in an actual professional development workshop. It was clear that they were mostly straight shots and that the thought of viewing the problem from a social-relational perspective was foreign and practically inconceivable. They wanted more business as usual—mini-lessons and other instructional strategies; and the principal acquiesced. For the remainder of my tenure at that school, we never had another professional development workshop oriented toward relationship-building. After I left the school, according to several of the staff members, the long-shot students took it over, and the place became more chaotic then ever.

When taking into consideration all of the obstacles and impediments that must be overcome to get into teaching, the low pay (which is about the same as a police officer, prison guard, and other non-college graduates in the private sector), and job expectations, the entire process appears fairly ludicrous. That is, unless you are the straight shot creating, implementing, and getting paid handsomely for constructing the system's programming. Furthermore, I don't think the system is designed to screen for the best and brightest teachers. I think that it's designed to screen for the best and brightest students—the straight shots; and the problem with that is that, as we all know, good students don't necessarily make for good teachers. Material knowledge and instructional strategies are not enough. If they were the key to change, we would have changed by now. Stop the preposterous charade, and change the approach.

Job #1 (Inspiration)

The most important and potentially most influential person that an underperforming urban student may ever encounter is you—the teacher. What you disseminate and how you deliver it could literally mean the difference between an abundant life and death for the urban underperforming student.

There may be those who disagree with me about this, but I fervently believe that the primary job of a teacher is inspiration. Let's face it. What else could it be? It can't be material knowledge, because all of the answers are in the textbook. In fact, at a certain point, students really don't even need a teacher to attain knowledge. In each and every discipline—math, science, history, and English—the questions and answers are readily available in the student and teacher textbook. Therefore, imparting material knowledge, albeit important, can't be the primary task of a teacher. Neither can disciplining students be the primary function of the teacher. Yes, as mentioned earlier, disciplining students is important, but it doesn't fill the void left in its wake after cleaning house. If anything, discipline and inspiration may be two sides of the same coin. And if that is the case, inspiration would easily be the obverse, or "heads," side of the coin.

Inspiration leads to encouragement, encouragement leads to motivation, and motivation is the first step that a student takes towards becoming personally responsible for his or her own education. Motivation is followed by skill attainment and culminates in achievement. Even though inspiration is tremendously critical, and especially so for underperforming students, there was absolutely nothing in the teacher education program or the district hiring process that screened for this trait—the ability to inspire. However, if I had to cite one single issue that impedes the learning process for urban underperforming students, beyond the inability of the teacher to develop a relationship, it would be the inability to inspire. Furthermore, the ability to inspire is actually a natural extension of the ability to relate, which, in turn, is the primary reason that many teachers can't inspire.

I can't begin to count all the times that I have met teachers, of all races and ethnicities, working in underperforming urban public schools whom I knew couldn't relate with, and therefore couldn't inspire the students. Many of those same teachers couldn't even relate with me. In one particular instance, the lack of relationship was so blaring that I finally had to say something about it. This woman was so afraid at the school that she wouldn't speak to anyone, except a few people of her own race, even when she was spoken to. At workshops, she sat with them; during lunch, she ate with them; and after school, she beat it out of there like there was a plague that swept through the community each day at three p.m. Based on my experience attending predominantly white colleges and universities, I would say that the teacher was experiencing a major culture shock stemming primarily from xenophobia. I told her that if she were going to have difficulty relating with minority staff members, then inspiring the students, who were more than ninety-five percent minority, was going to be next to impossible. Thank goodness she only worked in that particular school for one year. (At the present time, that same teacher is working at a much more affluent district school, and from all indications, she is doing a great job.) In the final analysis, I don't blame her at all for not being able to inspire the students at our school. She was simply a young, credentialed teacher who needed a job and accepted an offer. If anyone is to be blamed for this travesty, it's the district recruiters for going out and hiring people they like and get along with instead of people who have the ability to inspire urban kids. Urban underperforming schools need teachers who can inspire first, and then instruct. Inspiration is job one!

Conflict, anyone?

On each and every urban, underperforming school campus that I have ever set foot, and in each and every failing classroom that I have ever observed, it is the mismanagement of conflict that stands out like a debutante in a red-light district. In these schools and classrooms, the administration usually feels powerless to do anything about the problem, so instead of working to resolve it, they pretend that the problem doesn't exist. Or if all else fails, they revert to the old standby and blame the teachers for all of the conflict on the campus.

When I first became dean, students deliberately sought me out to see my reaction when they told me about the problems the school was having, and to assure me that there was nothing I could do about it. One student, with great exuberance, explained how students had thrown chairs at a former dean as he attempted to manage a disagreement in a classroom. Another student gloatingly relived a riot and the ensuing school lockdown. I was also told that the dean had discovered that a student had urinated in his coffee cup and left it on his desk. This school—which had two years to right itself or face consequences ranging from restructuring and declaring charter status to state takeover and even closure—was clearly having a conflict management problem.

As stated, I had never been dean of students before, and I had no idea even what the job description entailed. However, I assumed that being dean had a great deal to do with successfully managing campus conflict, which in turn created an environment conducive to relationship-building.

Initially, I wasn't certain about which course to take. However, I knew that I didn't like the system that was already in place. It undermined the teachers' authority, which resulted in very few, if any, being viewed as inspirational leaders and campus legends. All too often, I witnessed school administrators, counselors, teacher's aides, and even campus security staffers perpetuate the conflict between teachers and students by intervening like power-grabbing little moguls. What they often failed to see was that, if the teachers were not the leaders and campus legends, the academic environment would not be maximally embraced, the school would continue to under perform, the campus would become even more unstable, and their job security would be placed in greater jeopardy. If I could offer any advice about conflict management to the non-teaching staff members, I would say this: in a conflict situation, seek instruction from the teacher before you take sides or make a costly unilateral decision. The reason is this: the teacher has to reintegrate that student back into the fold, and the manner in which the student returns is vital. If the student is a long shot and returns to class in what appears to be a triumphant reentry, that class will probably be destroyed. The teacher's credibility, and any hope of relationship-building on campus, could also be shattered for the remainder of the year.

The first step in managing conflict is to identify, not ignore it. The next step is to construct and implement a plan to significantly reduce or eliminate it. And the final step is to insure that all interested parties embrace the same plan. In urban underperforming schools, I often see too many individualized plans in action.

As a final point on conflict management, in order to help people to identify it, I want to paint a picture of the conflict zone. Using the student profile graphic below, it is easy to see the actual domain of conflict. It is the area between the worst long shot and the least straight shot. With this definition in mind, it should be simple to see what the solution ought to be.

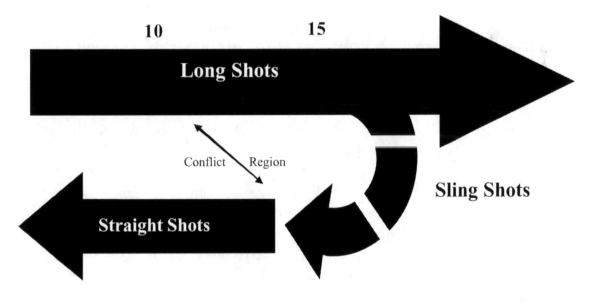

The key is to control the long shots and then get the sling shots to swing in the direction of the straights. By the way, it will also create more quality teaching time, which results in the filling of the negative void and an increase in academic performance, which results in higher academic performance index scores.

Get the Top-Dawg Syndrome!

Without being egotistical and arrogant, in urban underperforming schools, teachers have got to get the Top-Dawg Syndrome. That is, as a teacher, you have got to establish yourself as the ultimate leader of all of the students. I've seen so many teachers go into the class and become something less than the top dawg. When that happens, they pay dearly. Immediately, they lose control of the group and in some cases never recover. In this section, I want to offer a few suggestions for becoming the top dawg in your classroom.

The first and most important thing a teacher, or any staff member for that matter, can do to become a top dawg is work towards building an appropriately healthy social relationship with the students. Every chance you get, whether it is with a group of thirty-five in a classroom setting or with one or two individual students while out walking the campus, labor toward building the relationship. And while building the relationship, be sure never to confuse relationship with friendship. The students are not your friends. They are your students. You are on the campus *in loco parentis*. That is, you are the surrogate parent, not playmate.

Over the years, many of my peers have found my position on this friendship issue off-putting. Some have even challenged me about the attitude. I was once asked by a counselor, who obviously disagreed with my position, whether I had kids and, if so, did I feel the same way about them? My response was yes, and yes! I do have kids, and I do feel the same way about them. One of my two sons grew up with me, and the other didn't; that's often the way it is when you're from an urban underperforming, ghetto community. To the one who spent his childhood with me, I made it very clear that we were not friends in the traditional sense; no, we were not equal partners or "buddies." He was my son and I was his dad—the top dawg. I loved, supported, and mentored him. He went to school, got good grades, had as much fun as allowed, and followed my instruction. He clearly understood that I was the leader in our relationship. Even when he went off to college, as long as I sent him a monthly stipend, we were not traditional friends; I was still his dad. My son is now a successful mechanical engineer and, to this point, the only one of my mother's grandchildren to graduate from college. It wasn't until after college that my son and I began to work on developing a true friendship. As adults, we decided that we are compatible, and we recently became partners in a small business venture. However, every now and then, I still get a little top dawgish with him. He seems to take it all in stride. I think that the relationship is now based upon mutual respect and admiration. So don't labor on developing friendships with the students. They've got their own peer group. Develop a relationship via leadership.

In my opinion, the best way to go about developing a relationship via leadership in an urban underperforming school is to first become human to the students. Become somebody that the students identify with as being part of the school—mentally, physically, and spiritually. In other words, to be a top dawg, become a living campus legend.

The only sure-fire way to become a legend is to do what I saw the teachers from my youth do. They got involved with us. Mr. Banks and Mr. Fussell, for instance, appeared to live at school. They had a physical presence. They were the first people you saw in the morning and, besides Mr. Hammons, the janitor, the last to leave in the evenings. During the school day, in a very much disciplined environment, they earned their stripes by bringing science and math to life. And after school, in the extended day program, they demonstrated their love for us by being our biggest cheerleaders, supporting us in basketball, baseball, volleyball, drama, woodshop, and even cooking classes.

Even when they were not in direct leadership of the activity, they provided the spirit of relative peace and stability that comes with tried and true top dawgs and campus living legends. They were the campus beacons that provided the human illumination which was necessary for the programs to go forward. So, on my campus, that is exactly what I try to do. I set out to become a legendary top dawg.

I started by standing out in front of the school and greeting the students every morning (rain or shine) with a genuine smile. After the process became more of a normalized ritual, I started shaking a few hands, or giving up some dap (a handshake with a bit more cultural flair) to the ones too cool for the traditional greeting. Ironically, it was the long shots that seemed to like the notoriety that came with shaking hands with the leadership best. The straight and sling shots appeared to receive their satisfaction from the reassurance of my daily presence.

The next thing I did was to visit each classroom and explain my program, or my campus focus. While in the classes, I prayed for long shots to challenge my discourse. The challenges would be my opportunity to establish myself with the slings and straights and demonstrate the program's effectiveness to the long shots. Of course, in nearly every class, a few of them bit. And when they did, I promptly and politely set my discipline plan in motion. I would ask them to stand just outside the door until I finished my presentation. After finishing the spiel, I made a big deal about taking care of the problem students and instructed the teachers to send anyone else to me who became too disruptive to the learning process.

Long before teaching, I learned the hard way that when it came to disciplining long shots, there were only two games in town: fear or respect. As top dawg, or any other staff member, you shouldn't care which of these tools is used to get the job done. Both Mr. Banks and Mr. Fussell seemed to operate under this theory. Back then, corporal punishment was legal, and, when necessary, they dispensed it with gusto. For a while there, I was a regular recipient of their heavy-handed justice, and I grew to fear them. But as time passed and I became mature enough to see that their goal was to make the place safe for all, my fear morphed into total respect. So as top dawg, if students respect you, it's the ideal; if they fear you, learn to live with it for the time being. The important thing is to make the environment safe for all.

The next thing that I did, and would suggest to fledgling top dawgs, was to participate in activities. Participate in everything—a pick-up basketball game, volleyball, touch football, wall-climbing, chess club, anything, just participate. Whether it was in the morning before school, during lunch, or after school, I would find a way to participate in something. Even if I only got to take a couple of shots during a dead ball, or to quarterback just one play, or serve the volleyball one time during lunch, I would take advantage of the opportunity. Also, at nearly every school that I worked, I established a chess club. However, if you really don't have much time, or can't play that well, don't sweat it—just stand around and talk a little trash about the game, then move on. It nurtures the relationship.

It is imperative that you get out there and relate. There is no way around it. I've known principals and teachers who have tried every other way possible to get a buy-in. I've seen them hand out cookies and candy bars, boom boxes, bicycles, computers, and even cash money. But it did nothing to build a solid campus relationship. In fact, I think that giving students stuff in urban underperforming schools is actually counter-productive. As stated, my mom and dad were separated. So naturally, my mom had a few male suitors who would try to ease in on her. As kids, we hated the ones who came bearing gifts. Sure, we would take their money and other trinkets, but we knew they were bribes. However, the guys we liked and respected, and who reached top dawg status with us, were the ones who developed a genuine relationship. And, in my case, there was only one: Mr. Willie Lee Russell. He would let me help him change the oil in his car and allow me to stand around with the guys when a couple of his male buddies came over; and, as he was a truck driver, he took me to work with him a couple of times to show me what it was like. He reached legendary status, and it cost him nothing but a little time. So get out and become a top dawg.

Early on in my career, I overheard two young teachers talking about how to deal with urban underperforming students. One teacher told the other not to talk down to students in a condescending manner. I thought that was good advice. No one should speak condescendingly to anyone else. Nevertheless, as the conversation continued, I became more and more uneasy. Next she told the other teacher it was also important to physically get down on the student's level when talking to them and admonished her to always make eye contact; that way the student wouldn't feel powerless, and his self-esteem wouldn't be damaged. After that, she said that when calling a student on a violation, you should make certain that you fully explained even the most minor reasons why you were taking action. The justification was that students from "schools like this" don't really understand boundaries and limitations very well.

When she had finished, I wanted so badly to contest the poor advice that I about had a stroke. Students in urban underperforming schools want to know that you are in charge and not being bamboozled by some weak long shot running some low-self-esteem con. Students in notoriously unsafe urban schools also want, and expect, to see you controlling the action, and not standing around playing fifty questions with some clown. By the way, the number one question to avoid answering is "What did I do?" It's really the beginning of a never-ending, no-win, circular argument. Also avoid discussion over the obvious. The kids are not stupid, and they do understand boundaries. So when they attempt to act puzzled and offer the "Who, me?" line, don't go down that road. Immediately place that individual on a TSMP worksheet and allow them the opportunity to address what they believe to be the issue. That way, you can get back to teaching, which stresses the urgency of learning and solidifies you as top dawg. If they still refuse to participate, send them to the dean's office. And if your dean is supportive, no judgment will be passed, and the TSMP worksheet will be offered to the student again. If the student continues to refuse to cooperate, as dean, I arrange a parent conference and send the student home until the parent brings him back to school.

Prior to the conference date, I invite the teacher to participate, but I don't mandate it. Hold a parent conference and after the meeting, reissue the TSMP worksheet. (After the meeting, I also try to spend some time introducing and discussing some of my relationship building strategies, like what it means to be human, the 3Ts, the difference between self-esteem and arrogance, and so on.) Upon completion of the worksheet, the entire process is sent back to the teacher for a resolution. In this scenario, the teacher gets to maintain power and control over the incident and thus, the class. The teacher becomes the top dawg, and the dean reiterates the message by showing support for the teacher's leadership.

If there is a non-academic concern being promoted by a student, top dawgs address them after class or after school in detention, not during classroom instructional time. Make sure to explain this point clearly in your class course introduction. It keeps you away from the time-consuming distractions and sidetracks.

In detention, don't argue issues as chastisements, but address them as opportunities to resolve conflict. Detention is also a great place and way to compile disciplinary documentation of your efforts to resolve the conflict and concerns. It is also a great place to make investigatory discoveries about your students.

Top dawgs must maintain excellent records. TSMP documents must have acknowledgements from the student as part of the certification. Make sure that the students sign them and that you file them. They are a running record of your interventions. What I inadvertently found, via the TSMP worksheet process, is that it is also a good way to identify and detect students who are having writing and grammar problems. If the mediation sheet is littered with a large quantity of spelling and grammar errors, that's the time for the teacher to enlist help from outside support staff. At our school, we had an after-school tutoring program. Students who were found, sometimes through the TSMP, to have low writing skill levels were sent to tutoring instead of detention. As top dawg, if your school doesn't have a student-student and a teacher-student mediation program, help to create one, and then use it.

IMPLEMENT
NOW!

After reading this book, you may be thinking, "What now?" With this in mind, here is a list of implementations.

1. Ongoing Administrative Implementations

> ➤ Immediately evaluate the administrative hiring and promotional eligibility process. Perhaps more ex-long shots need to be included.

> ➤ Immediately seek and employ ex-long shots to work in urban underperforming schools. They can turn the schools around fastest.

> ➤ Immediately begin training and workshops geared toward relationship-building.

> ➤ Immediately begin workshops geared towards teaching students from A to Z. (Training should be facilitated by ex-long shots whenever possible.)

> ➤ At underperforming sites, immediately lay out your desired campus relationship plan—culturally and academically. Include the ex-long shots in the leadership and planning; they are most likely to give you an accurate assessment of the plan and its validity.

> ➤ Don't finger-point and blame teachers for systemic relationship problems. The opposite of blame is responsibility. Take responsibility for the relational and instructional environment.

2. Student Implementation

> ▪ Immediately size up your campus breakdown by student typology according to long, sling, and straight shots.

> ▪ All over the campus, classrooms included, immediately begin introducing students to the tripartition of being human—spirit (conscience, morality, ethics, integrity, etc.), mind, and body.

> ▪ Immediately begin the process of instilling developmental urgency through the 3Ts—time, talents, and treasures.

3. Environmental Implementations

> ❖ Immediately gain control of the environment, layout, and climate. The hardest part of this effort is getting the adults to be consistent.

❖ Immediately establish campus and classroom rites, rituals, and jobs.

❖ Immediately develop an atmosphere of cleanliness for the campus and classroom. Don't be afraid to make a big deal about violations.

❖ Immediately force the issue of campus and classroom ownership by displaying quality student work, not junk. Get away from the posting of junk to preserve self-esteem. It doesn't. It promotes arrogance and low-quality performance. I'd rather post nothing at all than post junk.

❖ In the midst of a relationship-rich atmosphere, promote a professional academic standard.

❖ Create a teacher-first campus. That is, promote teachers as the leaders in the professional process and everyone else as the support team.

❖ Vehemently disallow aimless wandering around on campus and in the classroom. Confront it NOW!

4. Discipline Implementations

✓ Immediately formulate, post, and consistently follow a campus and classroom philosophy.

✓ Immediately create and implement a campus focus plan.

✓ Detention is the place to dispel and debunk myths and illogic, and to build relationships. Immediately create and implement a school-wide and individual classroom detention plan.

✓ Immediately establish, post, and enforce a dress code. (I prefer one without uniforms. I think it's better to get the students to wear their own clothes properly.)

✓ Immediately take control of the restrooms. Long shots see restrooms as their office of operation. Control their office hours. Be as extreme about it as necessary.

✓ Immediately create and implement a teacher-student mediation program.

✓ Immediately create and implement a student-student mediation program.

✓ If possible, make sure that your chief disciplinarian is an ex-long shot or a highly trained, highly skilled campus legend. I've observed situations where they were not, and it was torturous for the teachers, students, staff members, and the campus.

✓ Immediately train counselors to be relationship-builders. If this is not possible, eliminate them from the discipline equation altogether at urban underperforming schools.

✓ As soon as possible, all campus security staff should be eliminated from the urban underperforming environment. An overabundance of security is a sign of insecurity, not safety.

5. Instructional Implementations

▪ Take the state and district standards seriously, but don't get hung up on displaying them. Instead, insure that they are woven into lessons and don't be offended when asked to explain how a lesson meets the standards.

▪ Immediately implement policies requiring a course outline, syllabus, and flexible daily lesson plans. There are some people out there trying to wing it, and that is simply unfair to the urban underperforming student.

▪ Use a variety of methods and skills to improve and induce good academic habits.

▪ Use real-world (urban student real world) instructional examples and authentic, valid, and genuinely realistic projects as part of the class curriculum in every subject. These projects are great for campus and classroom displays.

▪ Use grading as an inspirational tool as well as an assessment tool.

▪ Immediately add courses to the curriculum that focus on philosophy and religion, and government, business, and the media. These courses should be taught at the elementary, middle, and high school level.

6. Teacher Implementations

● Immediately begin to think of your job as CIO—Chief Inspiration Officer.

● Immediately evaluate yourself. If you find you are not able to inspire, or if you discover you are actually afraid and don't think you can be an effective relationship-builder in your environment, seek help. If you find that you are too arrogant or too embarrassed to seek help, *get out!* You may be a good teacher in the midst of a bad relationship; pursue your true school niche.

- Get outside and study your environment.

- Immediately work to become a campus living legend.

- Immediately demand to be treated like a professional. Refuse to accept the traditional role of scapegoat. Confront every slight. Demand respect!

- Unless there is a general shift in the educational and professional philosophy towards teachers, get in touch with your union and support it.

- Lastly, learn to think and, if necessary, to act like an ex-long shot. In an urban underperforming school, it is imperative that you walk in the door as the "top dawg" and never surrender the position. Material knowledge is great, and totally necessary, but if you never get to share it, it's useless. As top dawg, you receive the respect necessary to make your delivery.

Any school district can unleash the power of the essentials at their urban underperforming school sites. Just remember to remain resolutely focused on the overarching principles of Relationships and Resources. Then target the key essentials.

Appendix

The Teacher-Student Mediation Model
The Student-Student Mediation Model

Mediation is a valid, viable, and reliable means of resolving and managing school conflict. Mediation is also essential to the creation of a fair and equitable school culture. Creating and establishing a mediation program in your school is relatively easy. The program I created and use was inspired by the VORP model. Although there are several well-qualified mediation training programs to choose from, I would recommend the VORP process. I favor the program only because I worked directly with the organization for over a year. During that time, I found the training to be useful, advantageous, and fully adaptable to the public high school setting because the bulk of VORP mediation cases involved teenaged offenders. For more information about the program, you may contact www.vorp.org.

The principal forms and the basic operational instructions for a workable teacher-student and student-student mediation program are included in this appendix.

The essential forms for a teacher-student mediation program are as follows:

1. A Program Introduction Sheet

2. A Student Incident Worksheet (two-part document)

3. A Resolution and Agreement Form (two-part document)

The essential forms for a student-student mediation program are as follows:

1. A Program Introduction Sheet

2. A Conflict Options Sheet

3.   An Unmanaged Conflict Illustration

4.   A Student Incident Worksheet (two-part document)

5.   A Resolution and Agreement Form

(A copy of all mediation forms—A through I—is enclosed at the end of this section.)

The Teacher-Student Model (TSMP)

Introduction

In the teacher-to-student model, the teacher simultaneously acts as a participant in, and mediator of, the incident. Because of this delicate dual function, it is tremendously important for the teacher to fully understand the mediation process, purpose, and goal. With this in mind, it is easy to see the benefit, and necessity, in having highly-skilled, well-qualified professionals involved in the training process.

The Program Introduction Sheet

The TSMP program introduction sheet is the first piece of program literature to be introduced in the process. This introduction sheet should familiarize students with the purpose and goal of the program. This orientation task can be accomplished in as little as one page. In fact, I recommend that the introduction program consist of one or two pages at most.

Like the VORP model, the purpose and goal of the TSMP model is threefold: to allow the teacher and student an opportunity to verbalize the relationship breach, to discuss ways to restore the failed relationship, and to lay out a clear plan for their future relationship expectations. The introduction sheet should also make it clear that the program has a restorative justice as opposed to a criminal justice agenda. In other words, the program does not attempt to locate and punish a perpetrator; instead, it seeks to restore broken relationships and lay a foundation for building a quality future relationship. (See Form A.)

The Student Incident Worksheet

When a significant incident occurs, the teacher issues the student an incident worksheet. If the student accepts the form with relative composure, she/he should be allowed to complete the worksheet in the confines of the classroom. If not, the student should be sent to the vice-principal, the dean of students, or the designated mediation specialist to complete the form.

On the front of the worksheet, three primary inquiries should be made. First, it should ask the student to explain the incident from their perspective. Second, it should ask the student to offer suggestions for resolving the issue. And third, it should ask the student to communicate how they intend to conduct themselves once the incident has been resolved. The reverse side of the form should contain a section where the student is allowed to ask the teacher clarifying questions and express their personal comments about the ordeal. This side of the form should also contain an area for administrator or staff notes. In the staff notes section, the dean of students or other administrative designee should provide a brief explanation of the processing of the incident. For example, "The student incident worksheet was completed in the dean's office, and a parent conference was scheduled." Or, "After completing the worksheet, the student was referred to the counseling office." When the student has finished the worksheet and the administrator or designee has entered processing notes, the form is returned to the teacher for a response and resolution. (See Forms B and C.)

The Teacher-Staff Response and Resolution Sheet

When the teacher receives a student worksheet, the mediation response process is triggered. This response process requires the completion of the Teacher-Staff Response and Resolution Form D. In the response, the teacher (or staff member, if applicable) must first read and give consideration to the student's worksheet. (The currently-used school referral process, which only allowed for a statement from the teacher, was part of the problem because, in the resolution process, it did not allow for a mutual interchange.)

After contemplating the worksheet, the teacher then completes Form D, a three-pronged response. The response sheet includes sections that afford the teacher the opportunity to explain the incident from their perspective—facts and feelings—and then lay out an unambiguous strategy, which might include consequences for making things right again. Lastly, the teacher clearly communicates his or her future expectations for sustaining a viable relationship when reunited in the classroom.

When the teacher has completed the response, the student is mandated to attend a teacher-led resolution conference. The conference should be held after school and should not be treated as a detention or punishment venue, but more as a resolution venue. The conference is also the perfect setting for getting to know the student on a more personal level and discussing any academic problems or behavior observations that might be leading to the conflict. It is also an ideal time to secure useful, updated data like new telephone contact numbers for parents and guardians.

If all issues are resolved in the conference, the teacher and the student will sign the agreement section of the Teacher Response Sheet, and the completed process becomes a documented contract. However, if there are other issues that require further discussion, the parties move on to Form E. When all positions are satisfied, the contract document is endorsed. (Although it is not mandatory, a copy of the completed document may be issued to the student.)

The documented contract is the overt indication that the issue has been completed and resolved. However, in reality, the completed document also serves several other functions. Besides serving as a resolution and contract, the completed document is also a viable means of record keeping and evidence of a comprehensible school site intervention strategy. (See Forms D and E.)

The Student-Student Model (SSMP)

Although I don't speak in depth about the SSMP process in the book, this technique and practice is a vital part of the overall conflict management arsenal at any urban underperforming school. The SSMP strategy is actually a forerunner of the TSMP, and it is paramount to the creation of a safe, stable learning environment. Whenever the two strategies are implemented together as a practical means for conflict resolution, the campus instantaneously develops a culture and climate for peace and tranquility and, subsequently, learning.

In the student-to-student model, a trained mediator must facilitate the process. In a best-case scenario, because of the magnitude and gravity of the program's effectiveness to the overall success of the campus environment and culture, this person should be the principal, vice-principal, dean, or a person designated by the principal with the sole responsibility and purpose of managing conflict and creating a positive school climate (through the relationship building process). Again, although there are several well-qualified mediation training programs to choose from, I would recommend the VORP process for the training of the individuals chosen as campus mediators. You may contact VORP at www.vorp.org.

The mediator's responsibility in the procedure is to lead the students through mediation in a manner that is safe, sociable, and restorative for all involved. Using the program's education forms—the program introduction sheet, the conflict options sheet, and the unmanaged conflict illustration—the mediator must also educate the students about the process. However, the first thing that must occur is the building of trust between the mediator and the students involved. This is accomplished by the mediator as he or she subtly declares neutrality—or better still, actively declares concern for the welfare of all participants. After this has been established, the mediator must introduce the participants to the process.

The Program Introduction Sheet

The SSMP program introduction sheet is the first piece of program literature given to the participants. It should explain the purpose and goal of the program. This program orientation task can be accomplished in as little as one page. In fact, I recommend that the introduction program consist of one or two pages at most and that it take no more than five to ten minutes to complete.

In brief, the goal and purpose of the SSMP, like the VORP model, should be threefold: to verbalize the relationship breach, to restore the failed relationship, and to lay out a clear plan for future relationship expectations. The introduction sheet also should make it clear that the program is a restorative justice model as opposed to a criminal justice model. In urban underperforming schools, most students interpret a process which involves adults as being part of the criminal justice model, and as a consequence are reticent about involvement; they don't want to be known as snitches. Therefore, it is important that the students know we are not seeking to locate and punish a perpetrator, but we are instead seeking to restore and lay the foundation for building quality relationships. (See Form F.)

The Conflict Options Sheet

After introducing the students to the program, I always explain the four options for handling conflict. In option #1, whether it is real or imagined, one person has all of the power and exercises it in a tyrannical fashion, while the other individual suffers his wrath. The problem here is obvious. In the tyrannical model, eventually the individual being oppressed rebels. The counter action normally leads to the second option. In option #2, power is usually stripped away from the tyrant and placed in the hands of an outside source. In the public sector, this outside source is often the police and then a judge. In the school setting, it's the teacher, dean, vice-principal, campus police, and so on. While option #2 is superior to option #1, option #3 is even better. Option #3 is the handling of problems through conflict mediation. The difference between option #2 and #3 is that equal power is given to both individuals, and the mediator becomes a facilitator of the resolution forged by the participants. Option #4, which happens to be the very best way to manage conflict, allows both parties to equitably share the power and resolve their own conflict without assistance. After explaining the four options for handling conflict, I always ask the students to identify the option that they prefer. Inevitably, they choose the best option. (See Form G.)

The Unmanaged Conflict Illustration

The Unmanaged Conflict Illustration is to be used as an illustration to encourage students to buy into the mediation process. It is also a great teaching tool for helping students who are more visual and/or logical sequential thinkers understand what they have been experiencing and why they continue to repeat the cycle. With this in mind, after the introduction to the mediation process and after explaining the idea of the four ways for handling conflict, I then discuss the five steps of the unmanaged conflict cycle. The steps include anxiety or tension, uncertainty or role dilemma, inequality or injustice collection, altercation or confrontation, and modification or adjustments. When the sequence has been thoroughly discussed, I attempt to stress the urgency and importance to the students of breaking the cycle and restoring healthy relationships. (See Form H.)

The Student Incident Worksheet

As a way of streamlining the process and creating continuity and greater familiarity, the student form used in the SSMP is the exact same form as in the TSMP. The only difference is in the implementation of the process. In the SSMP, the students involved in the conflict work through the worksheet section by section with the mediator facilitating as a thought framer and process navigator.

As thought framer and navigator, the mediator's role is to insure that each element—verbalizing the relationship breach, restoring relations, and agreeing on future relationship expectations—is thoroughly fleshed out in a respectful and positive manner en route to a fair and reasonable resolution. (See Forms B and C.)

The Resolution and Agreement Form

The pinnacle of success in a SSMP is a just, equitable, and fair resolution and agreement. The agreement, which should contain an explanation of how the conflict was resolved and a section that clearly sets the framework for future interaction, should be documented, agreed upon, signed, and witnessed. A copy of the document should be issued to each participant. In addition, a file folder consisting of the used worksheets and the original agreement should be created and maintained for future reference. The resolution and agreement document serves three basic functions. First and foremost, the agreement document serves as proof that a workable resolution was reached between the student participants. Next, the completed file and agreement document serve as a viable means of record keeping; and third, the document is evidence of a comprehensible school site intervention strategy. (See Form I.)

VORP Inspired

Teacher-Student Mediation Program

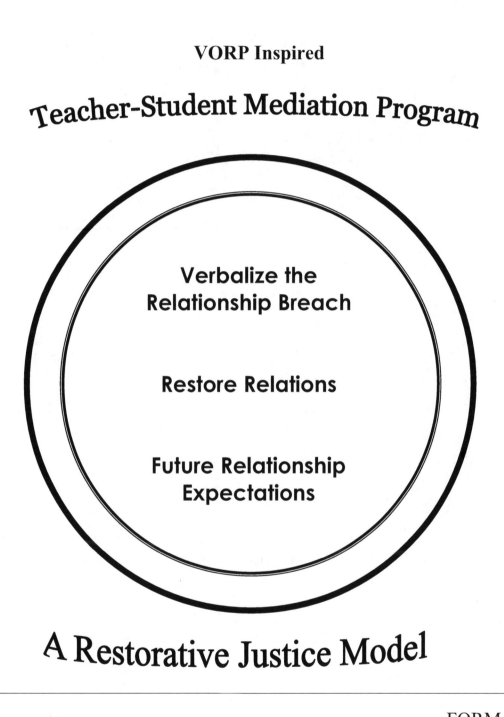

Verbalize the Relationship Breach

Restore Relations

Future Relationship Expectations

A Restorative Justice Model

FORM A

By Julius Lockett; August 20, 2005

STUDENT
INCIDENT WORKSHEET

Name _____ **Incident Date** _____ **Time / Period** _____ **AM/PM**

In your own words, explain what happened?
(On back, write down any questions or comments that you might have about the incident.)

| |
| |
| |
| |
| |
| |
| |
| |

What would make things right again?

| |
| |
| |
| |
| |

If things are made as right as possible, how will you deal with this person or situation in the future?

| |
| |
| |
| |

FORM B

By Julius Lockett; August 20, 2005

Student Incident Worksheet
(Questions, Comments, and Notes)

List any questions that you may have about the conflict/incident.
(Remember, questions begin with **W**ho, **W**hat, **W**hen, **W**here, **W**hy, **H**ow, **D**id and other interrogatories.)

1.	
2.	
3.	
4.	
5.	
6.	
7.	
8.	
9.	
10.	

Comments:
(You may respectfully say anything you like because comments don't require a response.)

Administrator/Staff Notes:

FORM C

By Julius Lockett; August 20, 2005

Teacher / Staff Response and Resolution Sheet

Responder _____ Date _____

Student _____ Incident Date _____

In reply to your correspondence:

Facts (what happened, response to questions, etc.):
Feelings (the effects and affects that occurred as a result of the incident):

Making things right again will require the following measures:

My future expectations are as follows:

Is more discussion needed?   Yes ☐   No ☐

If all positions are now clarified, please endorse below.

Signatures of Agreement

_____ Date _____

_____ Date _____

Witness _____ Date _____

Witness _____ Date _____

FORM D

By Julius Lockett; August 20, 2005

Teacher / Staff Response and Resolution Sheet

Please list the items that require discussion and clarification:

1.	
2.	
3.	
4.	
5.	

Discussion and Resolution:

As a result of the continued discussion, are all positions now clarified?   Yes ☐   No ☐

Signatures of Agreement

_____ Date _____

_____ Date _____

Witness _____ Date _____

Witness _____ Date _____

FORM E

By Julius Lockett; August 20, 2005

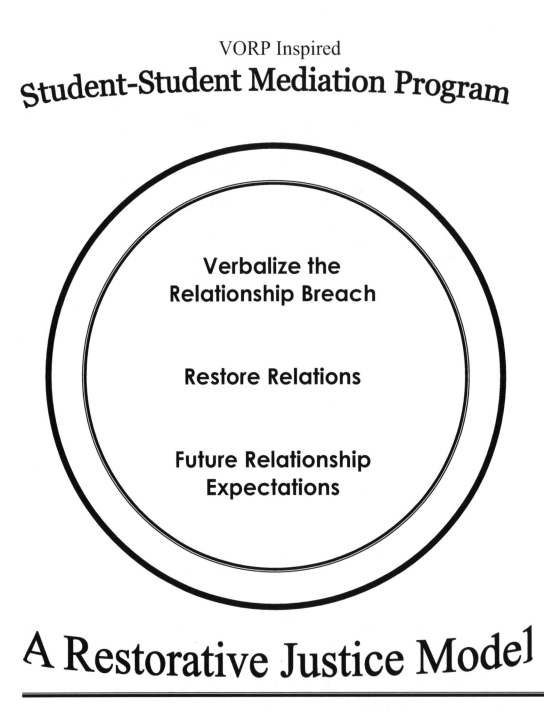

VORP Inspired
Student-Student Mediation Program

**Verbalize the
Relationship Breach**

Restore Relations

**Future Relationship
Expectations**

A Restorative Justice Model

FORM F

By Julius Lockett; August 20, 2005

VORP Inspired
Options for Handling Conflict

(The Four Options for Handling Conflict)

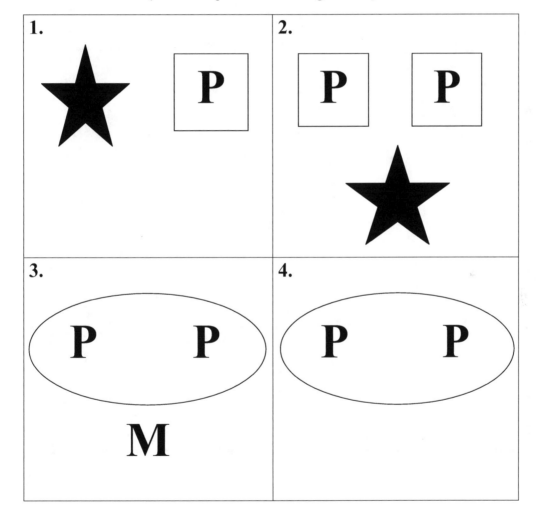

FORM G

VORP Inspired

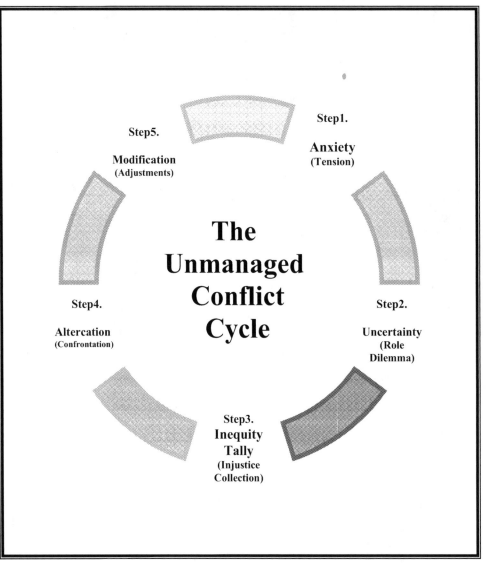

The Unmanaged Conflict Cycle

Step1.
Anxiety
(Tension)

Step2.
Uncertainty
(Role Dilemma)

Step3.
Inequity Tally
(Injustice Collection)

Step4.
Altercation
(Confrontation)

Step5.
Modification
(Adjustments)

FORM H

By Julius Lockett; August 20, 2005

RESOLUTION & AGREEMENT

The Persons Listed Have Recognized And Resolved Their Differences.

Print Names(s): _____

_____

_____

_____

Things were made right by taking the following measures:

In the future, we agree to do the following:

Signatures and Celebrations

_____ Date _____

_____ Date _____

Witness _____ Date _____

Witness _____ Date _____

FORM I

By Julius Lockett; August 20, 2005

Bio Sketch: JULIUS R. LOCKETT

As a youth, Julius R. Lockett attended Pryor Street Elementary School, Walter Leonard Parks Middle School, and George Washington Carver Vocational High School in Atlanta, Georgia, all of which were urban-poor underperforming schools.

Julius received a Bachelor of Science in 1983 and a Master of Science in 1986 in Public and Urban Affairs from Georgia State University. After graduation in 1986, he worked as a police officer with the Fulton County Police Department in Atlanta, Georgia, until 1995. In January of 1996, Julius was employed as Mediations Case Manager with the Victim Offender Reconciliation Program (VORP) in Fresno, CA. While working with VORP, Julius began work on a California Teaching Credential at Fresno Pacific University. He completed the program in 1997. For the 1997-1998 school year, Julius was employed as a history and language arts teacher with the Fresno County Office of Education and worked at the Elkhorn Correctional (Boot Camp) Facility.

In 1998, Julius accepted a teaching position with San Diego Unified School District. During his tenure in San Diego, Julius has worked as a social sciences teacher in alternative, underperforming school settings. The schools include Youth Opportunities Unlimited (YOU) and Alternative Learning for Behavior and Attitude (ALBA), the district's zero-tolerance community day school. Julius is currently employed as Dean of Student Success at Samuel Gompers High School.

While in San Diego, Julius received a Professional Clear California Teaching Credential in social sciences, and he also attended the University of California San Diego, where he obtained a Cross-Cultural, Language and Academic Development Certificate.

AWARDS:

Georgia State University: Regent Scholarship Recipient, Graduate Program

Fresno Pacific University: Teacher Education Academic Scholarship Recipient

Alternative Learning for Behavior and Attitude School (ALBA): Site Teacher of the Year 2002

Central California Dispute Resolution Association Award Winner 1998

Seminar and Workshop Contacts:

Julius R. Lockett
Telephone: (619) 276-4987
E-mail: jlockett@sdcoe.k12.ca.us
Website: www.ue101.com